MY LIFE MY HAPPINESS

Improve the quality of your life
in 16 weeks

A week by week self-care journal
for girls aged 11 and up

Nicola Locke
Created from her Empowerment Workshops

First published in Great Britain in 2020

© 2020 by Nicola Locke

All rights reserved

No part of this publication may be reproduced, stored in a retrieval system, or transmitted, in any form or by any means, without the prior permission, in writing, by the author.

This book is dedicated to all the girls who have inspired me throughout my life. I started mentoring young girls when I was 16, so there are many of you. More recently, the girls who came to my workshops and trusted in me have strengthened my desire to help others. I always knew that there was a shortage of support, but it was you that made me realise how important it was to write a book, to reach out to as many girls as possible. Your enthusiasm and commitment, not only to turn up every week but to complete the tasks and share your experiences made me realise the workshops were working. I have seen many smiling faces, transformed faces, grateful faces. For me, this has been invaluable, and I am honoured to have met all of you. Thank you to those who, despite feeling nervous on the first day, came along anyway. And to those who were not sure they could manage to stay for the duration, but stayed until the very end, thank you for taking that brave step into the unknown. I know from your testimonials how much you got out of the workshops, and with those priceless words you have paved the way for others to follow. I hope that having a copy of this book will keep you motivated and remind you of your wonderful selves.

It was through all of the girls in my life that this book was born, and I am eternally grateful. I hope this book will travel far and wide. I look forward to working with you and hearing about your journey.

Contents

CONTENTS	4
INTRODUCTION	1
ABOUT THIS BOOK	3
Stories from the Workshops	9
WEEK 1: MEDITATION AND BREATHING	**14**
Meditation Exercise	16
Tasks for the week	19
Creating your space	22
A word from your mentor	24
WEEK 2: SELF EVALUATION	**26**
Task for the week	31
A word from your mentor	33
WEEK 3: POSITIVE ME	**34**
Positivity list	35
Task for the week	38
A word from your mentor	40
WEEK 4: GRATITUDE AND WHY IT MATTERS	**41**
Make a gratitude jar	44
Showing your gratitude	45
Task for the week	49
A word from your mentor	50
WEEK 5: JUST SAY NO!	**52**
Signs of emotional bullying	53
Physical bullying	54
Gossiping and banter	56
Next task: Imaginary situation	64

A word from your mentor	67

WEEK 6: WHAT MAKES A GOOD FRIEND? 68

Task for the week	73
A word from your mentor	74

WEEK 7: HEALTHY MINDS 76

Chart	79
Thought chart	81
Task for the week	83
A word from your mentor	84

WEEK 8: KINDNESS AND HAPPINESS 85

Random acts of kindness	91
Task for the week	94
A word from your mentor	96

WEEK 9: SMARTPHONE CHALLENGE 97

Task for the week	102
A word from your mentor	104

WEEK 10: UNDERSTANDING SEXTING AND GROOMING 106

What is sexting?	107
Questionnaire	109
Task for the week	112
A word from your mentor	114

WEEK 11: TAKING CARE OF ME 117

Task for the week	120
A word from your mentor	122

WEEK 12: INSPIRATIONAL PEOPLE, POWERFUL ME! 123

Task for the week	126
A word from your mentor	127

WEEK 13: STRESS, ANXIETY AND DEPRESSION 130

Stress	131
Anxiety	132

Depression	134
Self harm	135
Questionnaire	137
Task for the week	141
A word from your mentor	143

Week 14: Healthy eating, sleeping and exercise! — 144

Task for the week	151
A note from your mentor	152

Week 15: My values and why they are important — 155

Task for the week	161
A word from your mentor	162

Week 16: Bringing it together with my vision board — 163

Task going forward	167
A word from your mentor	168

About the Author — 170

Resources: — 172

Acknowledgements: — 175

Introduction

Dear Girls,

My name is Nicola and I will be your mentor during your time using this book. This is your private book. Write freely and express your emotions. No one else has to read it. You are entitled to your privacy.

Before we get started, an important message that I hope none of you need, but some of you might: If at any time in your life you have harmed yourself, or if you ever feel at all in danger of doing so, PLEASE seek help. You can call Childline on 0800 1111, and you can find more helplines at the back of this book. Please reach out. You don't need to go through it alone. You may not feel like asking for help, but keeping yourself safe is an absolute priority.

It is vital to understand that when you find yourself stuck in a negative spiral, it is sometimes impossible to see your way out of it alone. Your thoughts can play tricks with you when you are feeling low. They can also be extremely powerful. That's why it is always good to share them with someone you trust. If you don't have someone like that in your day-to-day life, then please call someone who can help you see through the fog. There are many caring people out in the world. They are waiting at the end of a phone line 24 hours a day. Make them your go-to.

Be brave and be strong. You have so much to give. Don't let anyone else, or the thoughts in your own head, tell you otherwise. Those thoughts are not facts. They are beliefs. And sometimes beliefs can be wrong. Talk them through with someone who does not live in your head. It will help you to untangle the problems that may seem impossible on your own. Also, if there is any person in your life who you feel is not good for you, whom you do not feel safe around, you have every right to tell somebody.

Call Childline: 0800 1111

About this book

When I was 12, my friend's older sister once said to me, "Your body belongs to you. Take care of it." I was really grateful to her for telling me that, and those words of wisdom have stayed with me all my life.

Although these words have helped me over the years, at the time I didn't fully appreciate this message. Now, after raising my girls and working with children for more than three decades, I have seen firsthand how girls have become less and less caring towards themselves and those around them. This is making them very unhappy.

I believe you all start with good intentions. But, what I have seen is that girls can very easily become trapped in a competitive cycle that they just don't know how to break. It seems that when girls gather in groups a mysterious thing can happen. A negative vacuum can develop where gossip and competition become the main topics of conversation. Before you know it you find yourself at a sleepover where all you do is bitch about others. It's worth bearing in mind that when you're not present, the topic of conversation could be you.

Through the workshops that I run, I can see that some girls are not aware of what is happening. Girls can be cruel without even realising it. This is because the 'normal' banter has become so negative. Girls are often so tied up in it that they are either unaware of how they are treating others or they don't know how to get out of it. Negative banter can quickly cross a hurtful boundary. It is harmful to you and the girls around you and, if it is persistent, it can cause the most terrible damage. Sadly, it can go on and on, becoming worse and worse over time. Believe me, you don't want to feel responsible for damaging another girl, and you don't want to be the one who is damaged.

The effect this is having on many of you girls is devastating. Especially sensitive girls who don't find it easy to stand up for themselves and girls who don't want to be a part of these negative conversations, which they feel are wrong. It is causing some to pull out of school, Many are feeling lonely and insecure. Some have taken to isolation and others to self-harm.

The truth is that if you were aware of the damage that is created by nasty gossip, bullying, competitive banter, peer group pressure, hating, trolling and bitching, if you truly understood the consequences and could see how poisonous it is to your and others' well-being, you would not do it. I honestly believe that if you understood how destructive it can be to someone's confidence, self-esteem and overall life experience, you would not allow this behaviour to continue. It could just as easily be you who is experiencing its devastating effects.

If you are the perpetrator, try to imagine if this were happening to you. If you are the victim, take heart that this programme will give you the confidence and tools to learn how to navigate the situation. And if you have taken to getting cheap laughs at the expense of someone else, then know that it is not funny. If you are a victim of unhappiness, isolation, peer pressure, self-harm, anxiety or any of the other difficulties girls face, I would like to welcome you to this book with all my heart. I am so happy you are reading this introduction, and I want you to know that you are not alone. Sadly, young girls just like you are suffering all over the world.

I meet many girls who are all struggling to find happiness. It is common to find girls who feel rejected by their peer group, or feel that they are not good enough for the world. But, please know that YOU ARE ALL GOOD ENOUGH! You have just as much right to be here as anyone else.

What's more, there is no one else on earth like you. You are unique. We were all made looking different from each other, with our own interests and talents, and that is something to celebrate.

Friendships seem to be an endless battle at your age. And true friendship takes effort. As you go through this book, you will ask yourselves what makes a good friend. You will also ask: "Do I make a good friend?"

You will also gain insight into how to care for yourself. Self care comes in many shapes and forms. It is a vital part of your happiness, but we are never taught about what self care truly means. In these times that we find ourselves in, it is so important that you all start to take responsibility for your own self care.

This book will allow you to find ways to strengthen your character and give you techniques and tools to help you grow in kindness, wellness and happiness. It will help you to survive throughout your life. It will also encourage you to support your peers. Over the coming weeks you will grow in confidence. You will notice your mood change. If you put the work in (which isn't difficult) you will get everlasting results.

My hope is that you take this book seriously and give the tasks a go. It is only when you do this that you will be able to see change and get results. You must take responsibility for your well being and happiness. Remember, it is your life, your happiness!

Now I want to share some inspiring news with you just to put you in the bigger picture. There is an incredible revolution going on around the world. Young girls and women are coming together in ways we have never seen before. It is so refreshing, and it can empower you. I hope this movement will inspire you to make changes. If you can change the destructive patterns that are happening in your world, in your schools, and on your doorsteps, you will inevitably create a better place for yourselves and future little girls to grow up. You need to be an example for them.

The problem is, there is not enough support out there for young girls. I am sorry for that. I apologise on behalf of your schools and your government for not protecting you and making it a priority to put your emotional and mental well-being first. It pains me every time to see girls suffering because of something that could have been avoided. I am sorry that your problems are not taken into account unless they are seen as 'serious'. I am sorry that prevention has not been put in place in your schools.

But the time has come. Change is happening without relying on these institutions. It is you that needs to make that change. You need to build your character now and change yourselves from within. You need to become part of this inspiring self-care revolution. You need to put your attention on the bigger picture. You need to change the way you interact and support each other and make your teen years happy and inspirational. You can be a part of that change.

This book is guaranteed to offer relief and understanding about what is happening, and teach you tools to change yourself and inspire the girls around you. If you follow the exercises daily, your life will change. A big statement, I know, but I have seen how these exercises transform girls' lives.

As I mentioned in the dedication to this book, I run workshops with small groups of young girls like you We work together to support and strengthen self-confidence. I also work one-on-one with young girls. This book is for those who are not able to join my workshops or come to my one-on-one sessions. I wish I could run these all over the country and hope that others will step up and run them with me. But it is better to do these exercises alone than not at all. Maybe one day, you will feel motivated to run these workshops. If so, I will support you all the way.

I have complete and utter faith in you.

Please always remember this. If your mind is filled with negative chatter, know that it is up to you whether you listen. If your friendship groups are gossipy and competitive, know that there are ways this can change. You can change your thoughts. You can be the change. You can inspire others with courage and kindness. You can step out of anything at any time. Learn to surround yourself with the things that make you feel good. Be brave.

I wish you all a magnificent journey.

You can contact me by email at any time.

With love and kindness, your mentor,

Nicola
hello@nicolalocke.com

"I have learnt how to be brave, how to calm myself in distressing situations. I have also learnt how to make others happy"
Evi, age 13 (workshop participant)

"I was given the chance to express myself and how I feel through something more creative through the journal. Also through the vision board."
Anonymous (workshops)

"I know that I shouldn't worry about things. This course has taught me how to find ways for clearing my mind. How to destress and I now know how to help myself."
Amelia, age 11 (workshop participant)

"I think girls of all ages will find these sessions helpful. I think young girls like me will find it so helpful because I did! And even if they are older they might not have heard of these things before, and it can help them now. The things I have learned have helped me to become more confident."
Kyra, age 12 (workshop participant and beta reader)

Stories from the Workshops

Before we get started, I want to share with you two short stories from the workshops I have been running, from girls just like you. The names have been changed to respect the privacy of the girls, but other than that these are true stories. I wanted to share them with you to show that things really can change, and sometimes change can come quite quickly. This book is not the same thing as the workshops of course, but all the exercises and techniques you will learn are the same as the ones that we all do together. If you put the work in, and follow all my advice in the chapters to come, I am sure you can make a huge difference to your life and your happiness. I hope you find these stories inspiring, and that they fire up your motivation for the work to come.

Lily's Story

When we're young, it's easy to live in the moment and enjoy the simple things in life. You can see it every time you walk through the park and see small children playing on the swings. I bet you sometimes wish you were still that age. As Lily was getting into her early teens, she was finding it much harder to just enjoy life. She was becoming very self-conscious, and less confident around others. I found out later, from Lily's mum, that she almost didn't come due to this lack of confidence. She was so nervous that she felt physically sick. Her mum managed to reassure and encourage her enough that she took the plunge.

When her mum came to pick her up, she looked in through the window and was amazed to see Lily with a huge smile on her face and having a great time with the other girls. This is what happens when we find out that the tough things we're dealing with in life are actually very common, and more than that there is something we can do about it!

Problems like lack of confidence and feeling self-conscious are not things we often talk about, which means we never know if others are dealing with the same thing. As soon as we start to talk about these things openly, it's a huge relief to find out that we're not the only one. Unfortunately, unlike my workshops, the book doesn't come with six or seven new friends, so instead I've included these stories from other girls, to show you that you are not alone!

Because Lily plucked up her courage and came along, she learned all of the tools and tricks that you are going to learn in this book. She learned breathing exercises, a simple meditation that she can do by herself whenever she wants to, and she created a beautiful journal that she can open whenever she feels she needs a reminder.

The workshops Lily came to are long since finished, but she is still using all of these tools. Life is never going to be smooth all the time, and when the inevitable happens, like a big fallout with a close friend, she knows that how she responds will have a huge impact on her own happiness.

So many things happen to us that we can't control, but one thing we can control is what we do next. When a friend hurts us, it's so easy to turn immediately to some other friend and start bitching about them. She did this and she did that and she's such a so-and-so!

The most important thing that Lily has learned is that right there in that painful moment, she has a choice. She could take five. She could go and sit in her special place, where she always feels a bit more secure. She could breathe in a certain way that she knows will calm her down. She could open her journal and write all her angry thoughts down, getting them out without them leading to yet more problems.

When someone upsets us, we often end up thinking about that person all the time. We're so focussed on them and what they did to us that we forget about ourselves! We're upset but we are ignoring ourself. It doesn't make any sense, but we do this all the time! Maybe it's because we don't know what else to do. That's exactly what I want to teach you. There are lots of things you can do to look after yourself when you get upset, and they really work.

Lily's mum tells me that the big smile she saw through the window shows up a lot more often these days. Maybe you would also like to smile more often. I would like that too, but I can't do it for you. It's your life, and it's your happiness. But I do know that you can do it! All the exercises in this book are incredibly simple. The hardest part is saying YES, I know it's up to me and I'm going to do it!

Ella's Story

Most, if not all of the girls I meet in the workshops are dealing with similar problems. We just read how Lily was self-conscious and lacking confidence. With Ella it was low self-esteem, which is really just another side of the same coin. I'm sure you can relate. Her parents had recently separated, and she had moved school because of a very difficult friendship. It was all taking its toll and Ella was starting to have trouble sleeping. This is a classic example of how things can mount up, leading to new problems, and sometimes to a downward spiral.

Ella's mum told me that she was like a different person from the first workshop. Of course a lot of this comes from meeting the other girls and the work we do together. I would love for you to come on one of my workshops so you can experience this for yourself. But it's not just about meeting other girls. We talked about social media, screen time, body image, friendships and so much more. You probably cover these things at school but facing up to these topics outside school can have a very different effect. All of these topics are in the book and you can learn everything we cover in the workshops.

Ella started to feel she could make stronger decisions for herself. She began to take charge of her own life and her own happiness. For Ella, one decision was to stop watching a certain TV show that was toxic for her, and she was able to explain to her mum why she made that choice (it doesn't matter what TV programme it was — I'm not going to give you rules about what you should and shouldn't do. If there is a TV show that is bad for *you*, then *you* have to figure that out for yourself. You can do it!).

One of the things you will learn in this book is to start writing a journal. It can be so helpful to get all the thoughts out of your head and written down. Somehow it seems to get the racing thoughts under control. It works so well it's like magic! I hope you try it. Ella did, and it started to work for her. In the beginning the journal entries were very angry. Ella wrote about all her difficulties in life, which felt so unfair. This is great, girls! Get it all out. Better out than in! In time the anger settled down and the entries became more peaceful. You might find the same happens for you, but don't fake it, you have to be real in your journal.

Ella also made a cosy space just for herself, with cushions, a warm blanket, her favourite photos, a notebook and some twinkly lights. You will make a space like this too, as you work through the book. A year after finishing the workshop Ella still keeps this space and still goes there when she needs to feel safe or cheer herself up, but she has found she needs it less and less.

Ella has a friend who lives next door but the friendship has always been quite difficult. In the workshop she learned how to make a 'gratitude jar' for a friend. It's full of little notes, each saying something that you are grateful to your friend for. Last I heard, Ella hadn't given the jar to her friend yet, but just the act of making it has made her remember how special this person is to her, and has had a huge impact on their friendship. When she does present it the impact is going to be even greater.

Ella's life is not going to transform into a bubble of never-ending happiness, and neither is yours or mine, but Ella has learned a lesson that I hope and believe she will take with her for her whole life. When things get difficult, we don't have to feel like a victim of events beyond our control. We can step up and take responsibility for our lives and our happiness. It's easy to say that, but the only way to really learn it is to try it, and see for yourself that it works. If you work through this book I'm sure you can learn this lesson too, but you have to put the work in, girls! Don't just read!

Week 1:
Meditation and breathing

Meditation is a common practice all over the world. There are many straightforward techniques, and if you can find five minutes in your daily life to sit and be peaceful it will help you a lot. It is not often that we take the time to feel what is going on inside of us. We don't focus on our breathing, and we rarely try to silence our minds.

I encourage you to find a quiet space in your home where you can sit without any distractions. If you have your own bedroom, create an area in it where you can sit and be peaceful. You can make that space cosy by finding a comfy cushion or a soft blanket. Add some fairy lights and a little plant. Keep it available at all times and make it your own. It is your special place. If you want to take it a step further, you can ask your mum, dad or carer to buy you an oil diffuser and choose a fragrance that soothes you. Lavender is known to reduce stress and will help you sleep. Other oils are uplifting. It all depends on your mood.

Creating your space does not have to cost too much money. Pick up items in charity shops, or ask relatives if they have anything to offer you. Check out old magazines for inspiration. Ask your mum or a relative if they have any going spare. If they don't, you might find some in your doctor's or dentist's waiting room. If you ask nicely they may give you a few for free. You can tell them it's for a positive project you are working on. You can also find wonderful inspirational ideas on the internet. Try searching for 'creating a cosy space'. But the main thing is to try meditating. You can always add to your space over time.

Let's get started.

Meditation Exercise

Sit quietly, cross-legged if possible, preferably in a place with no background noise. I would recommend no music to start with. Quiet gentle music could be added later but, in the beginning, get used to your silence and be aware of your body and your breathing.

Close your eyes and bring your attention on to your breathing. Notice your breath. Often your breathing is shallow and usually makes it only as far as your throat or chest. Now ask yourself if you are breathing deeply. Your breath should slowly move down into your body, into your stomach. Your breath doesn't really go into your stomach of course—it goes into your lungs—but if you imagine it travelling right down deep into the bottom of your stomach it will help you to breathe deeply.

Place your hands on your stomach and start to take your breath deeper. You should be able to fill your stomach with your deep breath and you will notice this by feeling your tummy inflate and deflate. Take a deep breath in and out. Imagine breathing all the old air out of your body and releasing it into the atmosphere. On the in-breath, hold for a few seconds before breathing out. Inhale slowly, hold your breath for a few seconds then exhale. Do this a few times.

Now raise your hands to the centre of your chest. Place them on your heart. Now ask inside yourself for inner peace. Say to yourself: "Please give me inner peace". Now cross your arms in front of your chest and give yourself a hug, massaging your arms. Hugging yourself sounds weird, but it does feel good. Now, place both your hands back on your chest, bringing your attention to your breathing again. It should have slowed down by now. Now place your hands upright on your lap.

Keeping your eyes closed, I want you to bring your attention to the space above your head. In this space there are no limits, The space above your head is limitless and beyond your thoughts and your mind. I want you to imagine a safe place there. It could be somewhere you have been in your life, like a peaceful garden or at the top of a hill, watching a sunset. Choose a moment that brings a feeling of joy. Imagine yourself there right now and visualise how happy you feel in this moment. Rest your attention on this moment and embrace that feeling.

You can stay there in this silent happy space for as long as you like. When you are ready to open your eyes, lift your lids slowly and bring your attention back into the room. Slowly focus again on your breathing and start to take in the objects in the room. Make sure you feel grounded and alert.

How you are feeling right now? If you had to describe it in one word what would that word be? I would like you to write it down. Write it below in the empty love heart shape.

This word is there to remind you how you can feel at any time. You can add more words as you go along. Maybe next time you will have a different word.

Tasks for the week

Meditation

Do this meditation/breathing exercise every day for a week. These little things are extremely good for you, but you have to put a little effort in. Try to make them daily habits. I suggest you try this exercise either first thing in the morning or last thing at night. You can also try it when you are feeling stressed, angry, unable to sleep or overwhelmed. If you find yourself getting stressed, try to do this exercise straightaway. It will not only distract you from the current state, but it will also bring you back into balance and a feeling of peace. When you are relaxed and more in balance, making choices and analysing the situation can be done harmoniously.

> *"Meditation helps me when I am feeling stressed or anxious. It helps me so much."*
> Mollie, aged 12 (workshop participant)

A word on Breathing

If you find you are getting anxious you can use the breathing exercise to bring you back into balance. Check the breathing star for reference. This breathing star will help to guide you back quickly.

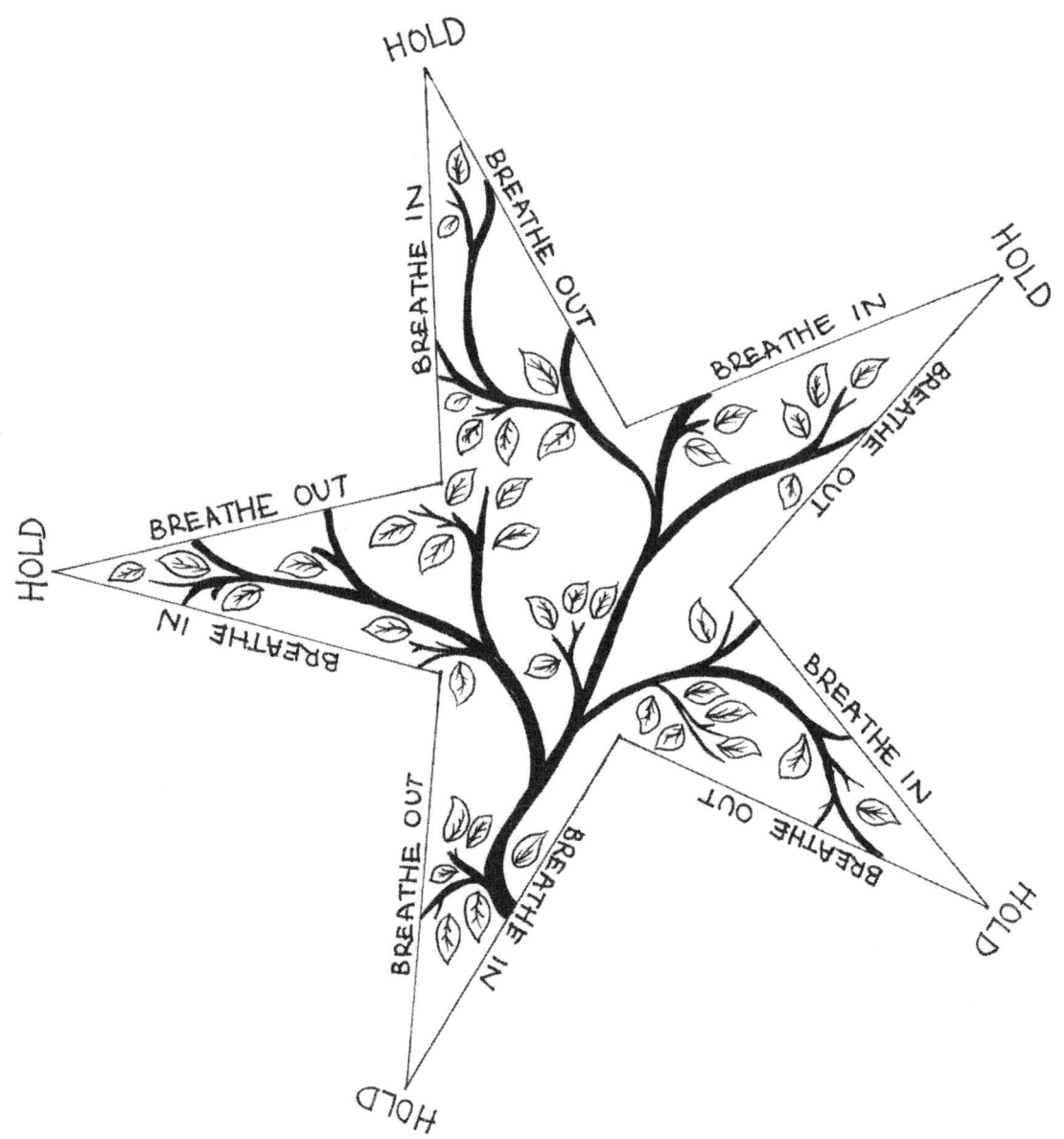

At the onset of any major stress, anxiety or panic, breathing is the first point of help. Focusing on your breathing will bring you back into balance. It will help stop you from going into a full blown anxiety/panic attack. Concentrating on your breathing will help you to self-regulate your emotions. It not only slows down your heart rate at a time of stress, but it also takes your attention away from your thoughts. It gives you something to focus on.

Meditation and breathing exercises can be used separately at different times. It depends very much on where you are and what is happening.

Creating your space

Use the space on the page opposite to create a collage. Use cutouts from an old magazine. You could draw, or print photos. What would your cosy space look like? What about smells and colours that you would like to have around? Think about what would make your space feel like somewhere you would want to go when you need some time by yourself.

My Cosy Space

A word from your mentor

As you go through the week experimenting, remember to write things down. Write in the empty page opposite. Writing things down helps you to see your progress. How much is it working for you? Did you notice any changes in yourself during this time? Keep a note of any changes that happen.

Girls have commented many times on how the meditation and breathing exercises have helped them. They have been of help in times of anger, stress and anxiety. Doing these exercises before bed has enabled them to have much better sleep.

Keep notes. If you find yourself running out of space to write, buy a notebook where you can write down your thoughts. You may also need it as you go through this journal.

Notes

Week 2: Self evaluation

This exercise will enable you to question yourself and your beliefs. It will cause you to question why you respond in the way that you do in certain situations, and help you to rethink your response. If your response is 'False' to all of the statements below, then this area of your life is clearly okay and you can move on to the next exercise. I would ask you to be honest with yourself when responding to these statements and remember that you are speaking to yourself and no one else. If you decide you are okay, it might be good to revisit this exercise another time. Wait a while before doing it again.

Which of the following statements about yourself are true? Circle 'True' (T) or 'False' (F)

I need constant self-approval from my family or my friends to feel happy.   T   F

I worry about the impression I make on others.   T   F

I will often go along with the crowd without questioning myself.   T   F

My appearance is so important to me that it can cause me problems.   T   F

I will do things that go against my values in order to be accepted by my peers.	T	F
I will not be seen talking to anyone who is unpopular, nerdy or a loner.	T	F
I judge others based on what they look like.	T	F
I find myself judging people who are different from me.	T	F
It is important to me that I am in the top set at school.	T	F
It is important to me that I am in the cool gang or group.	T	F
I would not dare to speak out in a group if I disagreed with someone.	T	F

If you have answered 'True' to more than three of the above it would be a good idea to address one thing at a time.

First of all, take a little time to reflect on why you have responded in the way that you have. You could use your safe and cosy space to do this. Ask yourself: why did I answer yes? Bring this question into your awareness. This exercise is designed to get you thinking about how and why you measure yourself against others.

When you have given yourself enough time to think it through, using the space below, take one of the statements where your response was 'False' and write down the reason that you responded in that way.

My reason: _____

_____

_____

_____

Take a minute to reflect on that reason. Then ask another question about your reason. For example, if you feel it is important to you that you are in the cool gang, ask yourself *why* that is so important to you. Then, keep asking the why question until you have reached a deeper understanding of why it is that you gave your original response.

My "Why"s

When you feel you have started to get a better understanding of yourself, you can flip the question and start to think about what you could do differently to start to become more true to yourself and others.

If you find yourself going against your values to fit in with a crowd, for example, you can question:

- Is it possible to help the people in my crowd see things differently?

- Am I able to speak out?

- Can I make a difference?

- Would any of them get it if I spoke up about the things I am not happy about?

If you answer no to any of the above you must ask yourself: do I want to belong to a crowd that goes against things that I value?

If you find there is a conflict between you and your friends, it would be a good idea to try testing the boundaries to make small changes. Your happiness is important. You have to make choices about who you spend your time with. It is not always easy, but you will find as you get older that you will drift away from people who do not respect your beliefs.

Task for the week

Start to become more aware of yourself. Pay attention to the conversations held among your peer group. Write answers to the following questions:

- How positive are these conversations?

- Do the people you surround yourself with lift your spirit and inspire you?

- Are they honest and loyal?

- Do they share your insights and beliefs?

It may also help to write down the names of your friends and question how each one of them makes you feel. Answer each of the above questions with a particular person in mind. If you start to see a pattern of negativity, you may want to address this and make some changes in the relationship.

It is good to remember that when you try to make changes for the better, it may seem hard to let go at first, even scary. What you will find is that when you leave behind the bad things, good things are waiting for you. Have faith in yourself. Be patient and be kind to yourself. You are on the road to improvement. It will all be worth it. Trust me!

Notes

A word from your mentor

What I often see is many girls going along day by day without ever questioning how they feel or if they are happy. Some do but are afraid to speak out in case of ridicule or rejection. I get it. I know under these circumstances things can be difficult, but taking a look at this stuff is really important for your emotional, physical and mental well-being.

If you do not address this kind of stuff, it can build up. You might eventually find yourself feeling full of sadness. It is much more healthy for you to address these situations regularly. The quicker you get in touch with how you are feeling, and get on top of things that do not sit right with you, the better you will feel in the long run.

"Happiness doesn't live in the place nor the cabin. It is in you. When you change they way you look at things, the very things you look at will change."
Prince Ea

Week 3: Positive me

Often in life you do not focus on the positive things about you. We all regularly focus much more on the negative rather than the positive things which are said about us. If someone throws you a compliment it lifts your spirit. If, on the other hand, someone says something negative about you it will likely stay with you for far longer.

Negative comments can be really bad for you. Especially if you have a low self opinion. People can't see what is going on inside your head and how you interpret comments that are passed to you. For some it's easy to brush off these barbs, but for others it can be a source of self sabotage. So, it is better to always be careful what you say to others. Choose your words wisely. You could be the reason that someone feels terrible right now. If they do not tell you, you will never know, and this is something that might come back on you one day.

Now, back to the positive!

This chapter is all about positive you. It's about looking at your strengths and putting your attention on all the good things. It's also about the positive things that others have said to you about you. Take your time while doing this exercise. Make sure you leave nothing out.

Positivity list

Write a list of all the positive things you know to be true about you. Remember to include the following.

- Things you are good at

- Things you are proud of

- Things others say you are good at

- Academic things

- Sporty things

- Creative things

- All the positive things people say about you. Don't leave out anything. It could be your smile or your hair. Whatever it is, write it down.

- All the things you have achieved

- All the difficulties you have come through

- All the things you do for others

- All the positive comments you've had from your teachers or school staff

- If you have a job, the good things your work colleagues have said

- Leave no stone unturned! What about the encouraging things your parents say about you? Or, what your friends' parents say about you?

Once you have carefully drafted this list, take a moment to reflect on it. Take a long pause to absorb all of these wonderful things that make you who you are today. Enjoy this moment. Allow that smile to spread across your face. I can imagine that you have quite a long list.

Positive things I know to be true about me

Task for the week

Make a collage

Having written a page on positive you, I want you to choose ten positive words that reflect who you are. These ten words should relate to what you have written. Cut them out of magazines, print them from the Internet, write them, or paint them. Use your creativity. Then put them in your book. Decorate the page. Make the words bold and make sure you include the best possible words that you can find. Make it a page to be proud of.

My Positive Word Collage

A word from your mentor

Next time someone says something nasty to you, or if you find yourself in a situation where you don't believe in yourself, I want you to sit down in your quiet space and open up this page. I want you to read your page with pride. Allow yourself to relish all the wonderful things you have written here. I want you to say your ten positive words out loud, reminding yourself of who you are. This is the real you. Whatever you think about yourself when you despair, when you stop believing in yourself, is not true. You have the proof here in front of you—that you are amazing! Do not let anyone, or any nagging thought, tell you differently.

ALWAYS remember who you are. Be kind to yourself. Do something nice for yourself. You deserve it xxxxx

"I love to see a young girl go out and grab the world by its lapels. Life's a b*tch. You've got to go out and kick ass."
Maya Angelou

Week 4: Gratitude and why it matters

We often go along in life not showing gratitude to those around us, or even to ourselves. Most of the time we take life for granted. It is important to pause for a moment and make time to think about the things we are grateful for and the people we are grateful to. The following exercises will allow you to do just that. They are designed to help you look at life from another perspective. You will not only find this deeply rewarding, but the people around you will benefit from this as well. Showing gratitude will give you a sense of bliss. When it comes from the heart it will make you feel so good.

Use these exercises as often as you can. They will most certainly brighten up your day and improve your relationships with others.

Write down a list of all the things your parents or carers have done for you since your birth.
Don't forget:

- Keeping you clean and clothed

- Time spent listening to your problems

- Outings

- Birthdays

- Waking up in the night when you needed them

- Driving you and taking you everywhere

- Cooking and cleaning for you

You get it. The list is endless, right? Keep going.

Now that you have written your list, read it back and reflect on what you wrote. Think about how lucky you are. You may not always find these relationships easy, but through all the ups and downs all the things you listed keep on coming.

At this stage in your life you might feel you want to distance yourself from your parents. You may find yourself getting triggered much more around them. That's the rebel in you. Most teenagers have a rebel in there somewhere, BUT I would strongly advise you to keep them close. Talk to them. Find a way to be open and work towards a trusting relationship. If you can't find this in a parent, try to find it in an aunt or uncle. It is very important that you keep the adults close if you can. Believe me, YOU WILL NEED THEM!

Things my parents or carers have done for me

Make a gratitude jar

Now, I would like you to find an empty glass jar. Any jar will do. Decorate this jar as beautifully as you can manage. Use coloured paper or old tissue paper. Stick things on to it using a glue gun, or a glue stick will also do the trick. Use old buttons or beads that you find around the house. Make a label and tie it to the jar. Label it 'THANK YOU'.

Now on small pieces of paper write all the things you are grateful to your parents or carers for. Try to use sentences and not just one word. Fold each piece of paper and place it in the jar. Fill the jar up. When you have finished, give this jar to them. This jar can be given to your mum and dad together or you can make one each. You can make it for your grandma or grandpa. You can make these jars for a friend or a teacher, your brother or sister.

Take a moment to imagine now how that person will feel on receiving one of these jars? Feels good, right?

You can make a jar like this whenever you feel it in your heart to do something for someone else. Not only will they benefit from it, but you will also get so much out of it.

NEXT!

Showing your gratitude

In the drawing of an empty jar, write all the things that you can do to show that you really are grateful. It's not just words! Here are some ideas:

- Help around the house

- Make my bed

- Make a cup of tea for Mum or Dad

- Clean my room

- Offer to cook a meal

- Offer to take the dog for a walk

- Help Grandma with her shopping

Add some more of your own.

Once you have your list you can choose one a day and make the effort to do it. If you can't manage one a day, try one a week. Whatever you do, make it happen. Write down below what you did. Keep track of it. This will make you feel purposeful and satisfied.

_____
_____
_____
_____
_____
_____
_____
_____
_____
_____
_____

Showing gratitude is a way of giving back and doing things for others. When we do things for others, we take the attention away from ourselves and our needs. This is good. It is good to take the attention away from yourself sometimes. It allows you to be in touch with others, and it allows you to think about others' needs. Helping out around the house and showing gratitude can change your relationship for the better. It is always good when something comes from you and is not imposed on you. Start to take responsibility and you will see how much that is appreciated. In return, great things can happen. You will be amazed at what you get back when you are giving from your heart.

Next!

Gratitude journal

I want you to buy yourself a little book or make one out of paper. It doesn't need to be anything posh, just a little notebook. I want you to keep it under your pillow with a pen (make sure the pen has a lid). Every night before falling asleep I want you to write down three things that you are grateful for from your day. This can be as simple as a cloud you have seen in the sky or a smile that someone gave you at school. Get my drift? It doesn't have to be anything big.

Task for the week

Keep your little book going every night for the coming weeks. Try to make it a habit. Give some time to this. Don't let yourself get distracted. Make it the last thing you do before sleeping. You could do a silent five minute meditation to help get you into the mood. Take advantage of the new tools you are learning in this book. Trying them out is so important. Even if you feel negative and don't believe they will work, fight that voice inside and say to yourself, "I want to feel better and have a more positive life. I am willing to try these things because if I don't, how will I know if they work?"

A word from your mentor

By writing down these three things, you put your attention on to the positive things in life. When you give time to these positive things your mind will rest more peacefully. You will fall asleep on a happy note and chances are you will wake up feeling much better. Evidence shows that if we go to bed fretting about negative things, not only will it keep us awake but it will make us feel awful. Don't give so much attention to the negative. Turn it around and pay attention to the things you appreciate. Focus on that and see what a difference it makes.
Keep a note of any changes that come.

"Showing gratitude is one of the simplest yet most powerful things humans can do for each other."
Randy Pausch

Notes

Week 5: Just say NO!

Emotional bullying

Emotional bullying is when someone regularly uses language to make you feel bad. If this is happening to you it can be extremely tiring and emotionally draining. It may affect your confidence, and if it carries on for a long period it can cause you stress and anxiety. In this week's session, we are going to look at the emotional side of bullying and see what we can do to make changes not only for you but for the girls around you.

Below is a list of behaviours that might be signs of emotional bullying. Some of these things may be happening to you directly, or maybe you are doing some to another person. You might consider them to be 'not that bad' or 'only messing around'. Although these things might be thought of as just part of growing up, you should also understand that if these happen too much, they could be hurting you or another person far more than you realise.

Girls are not always good at saying STOP. You might go along with this kind of bullying because you don't want to be the one to 'make a big deal out of it'. If you are one of those girls who finds herself in a peer group that is gossiping and using any of these tactics below, I strongly urge you to stop and think about it. Most of the time it is not funny. It can seriously damage another girl. If you are victim of this and need support please reach out and get help.

Signs of emotional bullying

- Deliberately ignoring a person

- Gossiping about someone behind their back

- Spreading rumours

- Using nasty comments

- Cyberbullying

- Sharing someone's private secrets

- Backstabbing

- Negative banter and insults

- Sarcastic banter

- Pointing out someone's weaknesses

- Mocking others for their small mistakes

- Laughing at someone instead of laughing with them

Physical bullying

Physical bullying is more dangerous and should be reported immediately.

Signs of physical bullying:

- Cuts, bruises or torn clothing

- Damaged belongings

- Violent threats that are implemented

- Stealing of belongings and money

- Forcing you to do something against your will

Young people take to bullying for many reasons. Some do it to get in with a clique, some because of prejudices, some may have been bullied themselves and want to get payback and others may be around violence at home and see this as a way of taking control. Whatever it is that drives someone to hurt another, know that it is not okay. They have no right to take their stuff out on you.

Although it is fair to say that people who bully are also suffering themselves, this in no way justifies the behaviour. But it does help to understand that people doing this are usually unh[appy and] don't know how to ask for help.

If you find you are on the receiving end of bullying, I wo[uld] suggest that you talk to someone and tell them what is go[ing on. It] may seem scary to talk about it, but speaking out will not only [get you] help. It will also make you feel less afraid. It will take the burden [away] from you and give relief that you are no longer carrying this alone. [If] you are being physically bullied you could be in danger, so you mus[t] speak with a trusted adult right away. If you can't go to your parents, talk to another family member or a teacher.

If you've told a grown up before and they haven't done anything about it, tell someone else. Tell them exactly what happened: who did the bullying, where and when it happened, how long it's been happening to you, and how it's making you feel.

Schools should act to stop bullying and should do anything they can to help you. They should also keep things private if that is what you want. Your friends don't have to find out that you told the teacher if you don't want them to. Say exactly what you want and don't be afraid. If you feel they are not listening, go to someone else. If you don't want to talk to your teacher, go to your head of year.

When you are bullied, you might be tempted to retaliate, but I would encourage you to try not to as it could make the bullying worse. It is far better to seek advice from a trusted adult. Always remember that it is not your fault and keeping it to yourself will not make it go away. It will have an impact on your mood, your work and your life in general.

If you find you are struggling with any kind of issues around emotional or physical bullying, please visit the National Bullying Helpline website or call the number below:

nationalbullyinghelpline.co.uk

Call free on 0845 22 55 787

...ng and banter

...o we say no to something so ingrained ...any just love it, and most of us have ...our lives. This message is not just for ...till doing it.

...many different kinds of gossip. You might start ...rsation saying, "Have you heard about so and so?" Then you may have a full-blown discussion about that person, telling yourself that it's okay because you care and you want what's best. But at what point does the help come? Does it come at all?

Then, of course, you have the 'no shame' type of gossip, where someone blatantly speaks about others in ways that is cruel and horrible. What I see and hear from girls is that you allow yourselves to do this because it is fun. You feel entitled to do this, and you go to extremes that are openly nasty. Sleepovers can turn into bitching parties where the whole night is filled slagging off others (who aren't there to defend themselves). Watch out for these. It can be really awkward to find yourself in this situation.

Gossiping can create nasty rumours and can leave people feeling devastated. It ruins friendships, it divides groups and most of all it is hateful. You might think it is just 'a fun bit of banter', but it can become extremely unpleasant.

At some point, you have to realise that this gossip and negative banter can be so hurtful to others that it becomes dangerous. If a young girl finds herself always on the receiving end of these unpleasant comments, it can make her feel so incredibly low that she may sometimes wish she didn't even exist. In the extreme, it may push her to self-harm. It is also good to point out that when we are cruel to others it is often because we are not okay. It is a way of being in denial and an excuse to attack others. We must be aware of this and make sure we reflect on why it is that we justify this behaviour. Is it to satisfy our own insecurities, and if so, is this making us truly happy?

I have seen firsthand that gossip and banter has caused girls to isolate themselves. It has prompted girls to leave school. It has pushed girls to cut their skin. It has led to suicidal thoughts.

It has become the reason that so many girls are living very unhappy lives. It is not okay to harm another girl through nasty words. It is not a joke that you can laugh at. Even if that girl never finds out what's been said, she can feel it. Continual sarcastic and nasty banter is dangerous and cruel, and the reason it is dangerous is because most girls will shut up and put up. They stay silent because they are under so much pressure.

I am aware that, especially in the UK, critical banter is considered to be playful and is accepted. The problem is, banter can become gradually more and more sarcastic, eventually becoming poisonous and causing no end of pain.

It leaves girls feeling a big lack of confidence, leading to shame and insecurities.

If you feel that negative banter is all just fun, then I would ask you to seriously question yourself. In what way is this fun? Why? What are your justifications for such fun? What is really behind it? If you are really honest with yourself, you might find out that, in fact, you are a bit hurt by the critical banter that has been aimed at you, and you feel you have every right to dish a bit out for a change. Maybe you feel you have been put down, and you do this to big yourself up again.

This next exercise will help you ask these questions. We are going to put it to the test. Once we've done that, I'm sure you will be asking for the next step, which is to find ways of stepping up and stepping out!

Doing this next exercise will help you to feel what it might be like to be a victim of emotional bullying. I didn't put this exercise in to make you feel bad, I just want you to engage in the emotions, to help you become aware of the consequences. I hope this will show you whether you need to make changes, so that you can stop taking part in habits that damage your friends and you.

Let's get started.

On this page I want you to write about a situation where you found yourself in a gossiping circle. It may have been many of you, or just two. Think about it. When did you find yourself in a situation where you were either listening or actively taking part in a negative bit of gossip? Who was there? Who did you talk about? Write it all down. Who instigated the gossip? Was it you? Did you join in? Be honest. Remember this is not a judgement exercise. It's not for anyone else. It's for you, a way to help you see what is happening. If you want you can write it on a separate piece of paper, and then throw it away at the end.

Okay, stay with me...

Now, having written that down I want you to put yourself in the shoes of whoever it was that you were talking about. Imagine her overhearing every word of that conversation. What feelings would she be experiencing right now? Try to write down everything. Try to think through all of the thoughts and emotions she might experience.

_____

_____

_____

_____

_____

_____

_____

_____

_____

_____

_____

_____

_____

Now...

Imagine a new situation. This time you are not in the gossiping group. You are the one they are talking about. Write down what you would be feeling if three of your besties were gossiping negatively about you. If your friendship group is anything like the ones that seem to be so common these days, I think you might find it quite easy to imagine. What would be going through your head right now? Ask yourself what emotions would be going on inside you and also what is happening to your body physically?

_____
_____
_____
_____
_____
_____
_____
_____
_____
_____
_____

The answers you are giving right now, this is exactly how others feel.

So, if you know you've been joining in this kind of negative gossip, ask yourself the following:

- Why do I do it?

- Is this how I want to make others feel?

- What do I gain from it?

- Do I feel comfortable about it?

- Does this go against my values and morals?

- Will I keep doing this?

Gossiping and shaming others can be done in many ways. Social media is a big one. We'll come to that later.

Now on the opposite page I want you to write down the things you could do to make a difference.

Answer the following questions:

What would you do differently next time you find yourself in such a situation?

_____
_____
_____

What might you say?

_____
_____
_____

How could you make others more aware of the negative effect this is having?

_____
_____
_____

Could you change the subject? How would you do this?

_____
_____
_____

Could you be more bold and take a stand against it?

Could you talk to your peers individually and get a feeling of how each one feels?

Next task: Imaginary situation

Imagine a perfect outcome for you and your friends. Ask yourself: what would make your friendships more positive? Think of all the things that you would like to see change in a day with your friends. What would make it a more happy and fulfilling one? List everything. What would a perfect day look like for you or any girl? Imagine yourself in the perfect friendship with others. What would that be like? Imagine how it would be if all girls were happy and supportive. Imagine a world where all the girls around you were smiling at you and making sure you were okay. It is time to turn this around. You can turn this around.

Having created this imaginary situation, think about change and how you can make change happen.

Sometimes it helps to list your friends and question what feelings each of them give you. Are they happy ones? If the answer is no, try to dig deep and ask yourself why. Try to come up with a solution that would make your friendships stronger and more productive. Think of ways to strengthen your relationships with others.

Could you be the bridge to getting your friends to stop this negative behaviour? Start by thinking of one or two friends you could talk to, and make a pact. Having someone else on board will make it easier. I can guarantee that, underneath all the tough talk, all girls want the same thing. They want to be liked and loved. You can give each other these things. It doesn't have to be difficult, but the only thing is it has to start from someone.

Despite all the difficulties, try to stay true to yourself.

My Perfect Day

Use these five rules often:

1. Never talk badly behind someone's back

2. Never take sides between your friends

3. Be the bridge-builder and help friends to make peace

4. Be kind

5. Listen properly and with a non-judgemental ear

A word from your mentor

Believe me, I know you have amazing qualities. You have so much to give. I see that every girl is unique and because of that, this world is colourful and exciting.

In groups something changes, and it can be difficult to go against the crowd. If that negative energy in a group is pushed by someone who is controlling, confident and domineering, then it will take a strong person to shake things up.

I believe that everyone can all be instrumental in changing things for the better, but your individual dynamism has to be used to support others. You suffer when you use your power to bring other down. You must not accept this. You could be lifting them up.

Imagine a world where girls' combined strength is used to elevate, inspire and ignite, to support and to be kind always. You have the ability to do great things, but you must be united. You need each other.

The world needs you to come together. Be the change!

"Don't let anyone rob you of your imagination, your creativity, or your curiosity. It's your place in the world; it's your life. Go on and do all you can with it, and make it the life you want to live.
Mae Jemison

Week 6:
What is a good friend?

Friends can be hard to come by. It can feel like no matter how much effort you put into a friendship, it can take just a second for it all to disappear down the drain. When fallouts happen they can be exhausting, leaving you feeling hurt and upset. Sometimes you will fight with your friends, and those conflicts can even leave you battling your own thoughts and beliefs. You might not always understand how the fight happened. You may go from feeling like you've got a good friend to feeling like no one cares.

Welcome to the world of teen girls!

Because girls are particularly sensitive and love a good bit of drama, things can have a tendency to become exaggerated and out of control. It's good to keep this in mind. Remember the calming exercise I taught you in week one. Meditation and breathing? This might be a time when you feel you need it.

I have noticed that friendships in girls start to change around the age of ten or eleven. When you find yourselves 'growing up' your friends often change as you move towards people who share your new likes and interests. For some, moving up to secondary school can be a big challenge, and it is often at this time that you are trying your hardest to fit in and be liked. You are trying to find your identity, and fitting into a group is important to you. This is all really understandable.

But in all this trying to fit in, it is easy to lose sight of yourself and your values, to get swept up in the whirlwind. You may not even notice what's going on. Your old friends might say: "You're not the same anymore." Life always changes. But whatever happens, remember to be kind.

If you find yourself moving from an old friend to a new one, do this kindly and try to make time for the old friend, even if it's less time than you used to have for them. It is important to question your loyalty from time to time. You will find that friendships keep changing until you find a group of people who resonate with your needs and likes. The most important thing is to avoid hurting anyone along the way.

Stay true to who you are and try not to go along with a group that doesn't fit with your values. If your friends take you away from your values, in the long run they won't make you happy.

Let's ask ourselves the question: what makes a good friend?

Here is an exercise that will help you answer that question. Use the mind map on the next page as a starting point to writing down all the things that come into your head. It might help to think of a particular person you know, or once knew, who has all the qualities of a good friend. You could even put a friend's name into the middle of the chart.

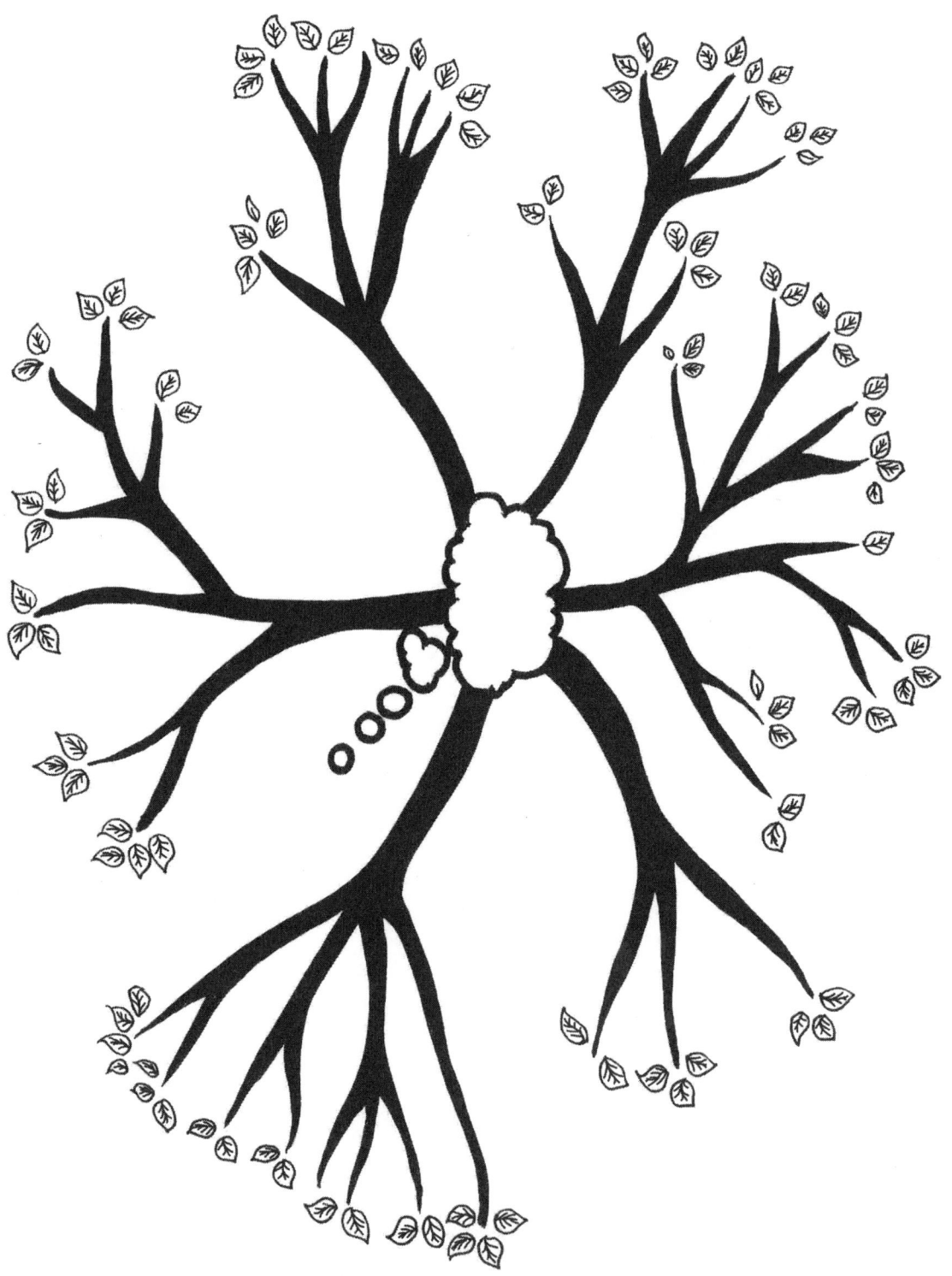

Okay, now here is a simple rule of friendships: the best way to have good friends, is to *be* a good friend. When you have completed the first mind map, use the second one to write down all the qualities *you* have. Do you have the qualities to be a good friend? Do you measure up? Don't worry if you're not as good a friend as you would like to be. You can change if you want to!

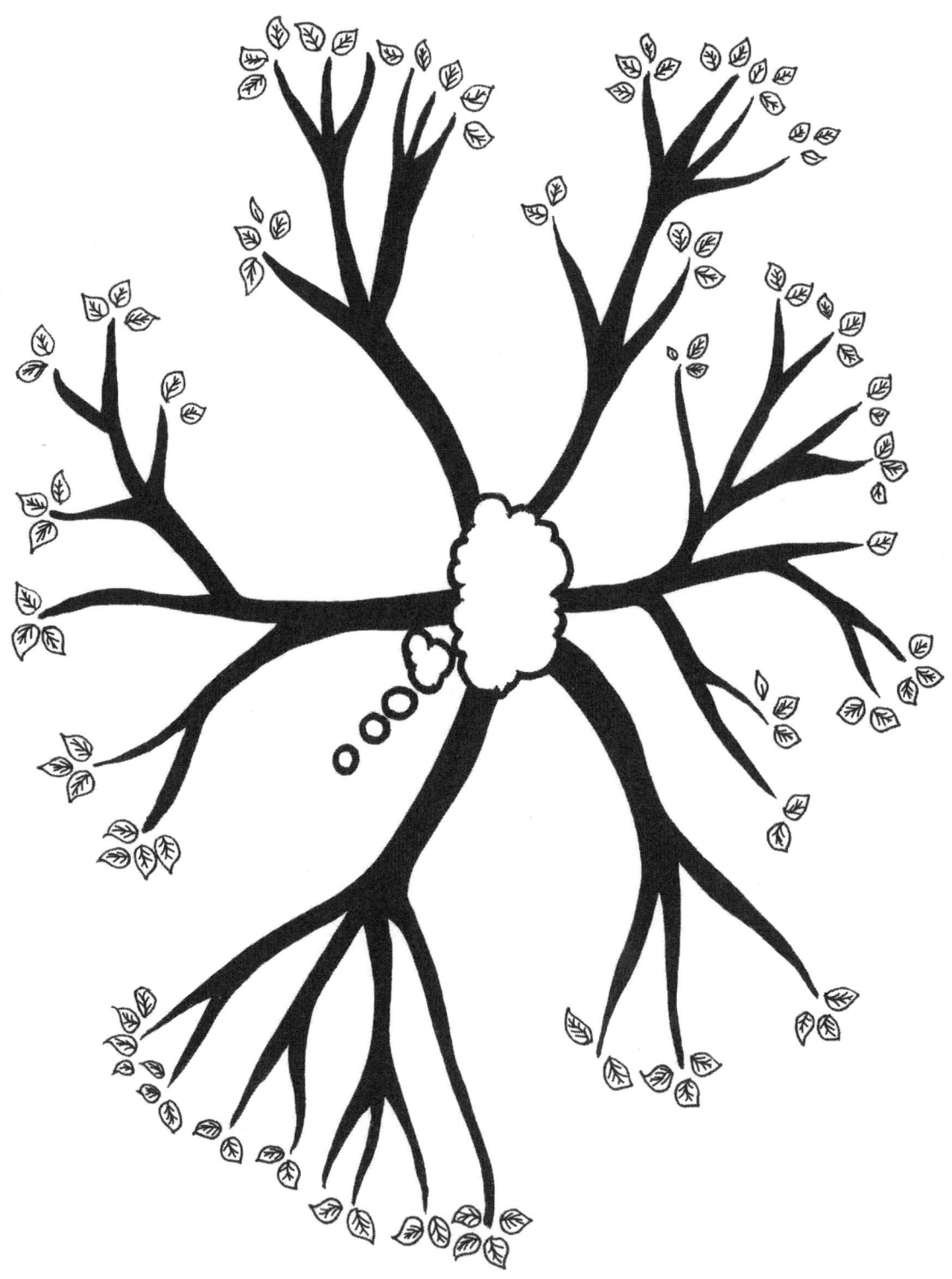

Task for the week

This week I would like you to do something for a friend. Create something just for her like a handmade card. Write a poem. Send her a letter. Bake her a cake. Whatever you choose, make sure you put a bit of effort into it. You could make your friend a gratitude jar and remind her of all the wonderful memories you share. You could give her a sentimental gift. This task can be for a friend you have lost touch with or someone you don't always spend time with.

A word from your mentor

We are often so busy that we forget to show each other how much we care. We go through life jumping from one friend to another, and we are often not too forgiving of a friend who may have hurt us. When you complete the exercise in this chapter it can spark a feeling of kindness in you.

It is important to stand back from your friendships and reflect on the good people in your lives. If a friend has been neglectful or hurtful, try to ask yourself what she may be going through. Could you help her?

Think about your friendships as something that takes time. You have to be a good friend to make long-lasting relationships. It's worth putting in the effort. Show your friends you are there through the good and the bad days.

Trust is a big one when it comes to friendships. If you do something that will lose you the trust of a good friend, you will find it hard to regain that friendship in the same way. Think about that before you drop your old friends for new ones. Try to be aware of others' feelings. It is always good to ask yourself how would you feel if your friend was unkind to you. This helps you to put your friendships in perspective. Sometimes you will have to let go, and that's okay. Friends come and go, but good friends will always find a way back

"I think if I've learned anything about friendship, it's to hang in, stay connected, fight for them, and let them fight for you. Don't walk away, don't be distracted, don't be too busy or tired, don't take them for granted. Friends are part of the glue that holds life and faith together. Powerful stuff."
Jon Katz

Week 7: Healthy Minds

This week you are going to think about the things you say to yourself and how your negative thoughts can affect you. You're going to try to become more aware of the way you talk privately inside your head. No one else can hear your thoughts, so unless you share them with someone, you alone live with them.

Are you kind to yourself, or are you sometimes cruel? On bad days maybe there is a continual stream of negative self-chatter. Often a negative thought can go around and around for days or even weeks. If you don't know a way to change these thoughts, they can be the seeds that eventually grow into anxiety or depression.

Happiness and sadness are, to a great extent, simply a matter of what we focus on. There's *always* something to be negative about, and equally there's always something to be positive about. When we let ourselves dwell on negative thoughts, it's almost like we are choosing to be unhappy. But with a bit of effort, we can change our thoughts, and change our mood.

Answer the questions below. Circle 'Yes' or 'No'.

- If you make a mistake do you call yourself stupid?
  Yes / No

- Do you find yourself having negative chatter with yourself?
  Yes / No

- Do you use a negative tone of voice in your private thoughts?
  Yes / No

- Do you feel things happening in your body when your thoughts are negative? For example, a tight chest, stomach tension, a dry throat, a hot and flushed face, or other feelings.
  Yes / No

- Do you find yourself thinking: I'll never be able to do this?
  Yes / No

- Do you find yourself thinking: I wish I could be as good as her, or: I will never be as good as her?
  Yes / No

- When someone says something cynical to you, do you find yourself allowing a negative story to emerge in your mind?
  Yes / No

Let's change it. What if you were to divert your mind to thoughts like these?

- This is a bit scary, but I'll do my best.

- They are just being negative. I'm not going to give it another thought.

- It's okay to make a mistake. I will learn from my mistakes.

- I can't be good at everything.

- No one has all the answers to everything.

- Life is a challenge. Each challenge is a chance to learn something new.

- Mistakes help me to grow and mature.

- It takes practice to get better at things. I can do this!

Chart

On the opposite page is a chart. On one side, write down five things you say to yourself that are negative. Now, think about what you could say that are more positive. Then write them on the opposite side. Use this method to get into a more positive frame of mind when it comes to thinking about you. Make it a habit to fill in your chart every time you find yourself stuck on negative thoughts. It could be a project you are working on, a piece of homework, an exam or a friendship problem. Get your negative thoughts on to paper. Look at them. Now change them to something more positive. Start to get into the habit of challenging your thought process. Say to yourself, hold on, I can think differently about this.

It helps to think: what would I say to a friend who was thinking negatively about herself? Imagining you are giving advice to someone else can be a great way to figure out what you need to tell yourself. Try it!

Start to become more aware of the thoughts in your mind. Can you notice when you are putting yourself down? Try to put your attention on this every day. Even five minutes of quiet reflection will make a big difference. Do it while you clean your teeth! It is up to you if you want to listen to your negative thoughts. Only you can change the thoughts that fly around in your head.

Thought chart

I want you to fill in the thought chart on the following page. This will get you to question your thoughts a bit further. Remember: *thoughts are not facts.* Just because you think something all the time doesn't mean it's true. It's just a belief that you have built up about yourself. Ask yourself a simple question: what evidence do I have for that? Be tough on the thought, like a lawyer. Prove it! Where is your evidence? When you test your thoughts like this, you will find many of them do not pass the test. They are a lie. You have to call these thoughts out and expose them. Filling out your thought chart will help.

A good time to remember that thoughts are not facts is any time you are triggered. By this I mean when someone says or does something that triggers a big reaction in you. When this happens, see if you can remember to step back and challenge the thoughts that have jumped up. You could turn to the thought chart every time you are triggered. You will start to learn how to stop negative reactions in their tracks. It's not easy, but it is possible, and it's such a valuable life lesson. These lessons are the path to a much more confident and happy you!

You can even be a bit strict with yourself. Tell yourself off! Say NO! I don't have to listen to this. I can choose to see this differently. I will not ruin my day with this negative self-talk.

Trigger	What triggered the thoughts to start?
Emotions + Feelings	What is going on in your body?
Negative thoughts	What are you telling yourself?
Evidence to support thoughts	Any truth?
An alternative thought	Think about what would you say to a good friend
What would be a more accurate way to respond next time?	Think about what you have learnt

Task for the week

This week I want you to keep the chart and the thought chart in your mind. You could leave the book open somewhere in your bedroom to remind you. Keep coming back to these tools and use them when you need to. The key thing here is repetition. The mind tends to run around doing its own thing, and it is hard to control. Imagine if your hands were as unruly as your thoughts! To change it you have to work at it, so keep returning to the exercises. Fill them in whenever possible. If you run out of space use a notebook to keep track of your thoughts. With practice you can change negative self-talk into positive self-talk.

A word from your mentor

Your mind is powerful, isn't it? You will see this for yourself if you follow the exercises above. How often have you told yourself something negative that you don't really have any evidence for? If you constantly put yourself down and give attention to the negative you will find it harder and harder to pick yourself up. Keep an open mind and examine your thoughts. Only you can change your mind. No one can do it for you. Don't rely on things going well to keep you in a good mood. See everything life throws at you as an opportunity to grow.

"A man is but a product of his thoughts. What he thinks, he becomes."
Mahatma Gandhi

Week 8: Kindness and happiness

"Happiness was always important to me.
Even at the young age of eleven, it was my biggest ambition.
People would ask, "Goldie, what do you want to be
when you grow up?"
"Happy," I would reply, looking in their eyes.
"No, no," they'd laugh. "That's really sweet,
but I mean … what do you want to be?
A ballerina? An actress maybe?"
"I just want to be happy."

Goldie Hawn

As we go through life it is important to do the things that make us happy, to be kind to ourselves and, equally, to others. At times, of course, we will find ourselves being unkind. We should take the time to think about why that is. Why would you want to be unkind to yourself, or to anyone for that matter? Okay, you may just be having a bad day, but you don't want to make a habit of it.

In your teens, the same hormones that drive the changes in your body can also leave your mood all over the place. You might find you are irritable and more reactive. Another reason you should take the time to ask yourself what it is that makes you happy!

The tricky part is not so much finding things that make you happy, but finding things that *keep* you that way. A packet of yummy sweets might make you happy—for half an hour, but after the first few you're just munching on them without really noticing, and after half the packet you feel sick! It's amazing how many things in life are like this. Even luxury holidays and designer shopping sprees get boring if you're rich enough to do them all the time. What's a girl to do?

Luckily, there *is* a way to make yourself feel good that never gets old. Being kind to others. It might sound corny, but it's true. Doing kind things for others makes you feel good, and not just today but tomorrow and the next day. You can make someone's day, leave them feeling extremely positive and bring them out of a bad moment, and at the same time do all those things for yourself. It works!

Let's get started.

In the first mind map write down all the things that are gained from being kind to others and being kind to yourself. What do you gain and what do others gain? What does kindness bring?

In the opposite mind map write down all the things that come from being unkind to yourself or others. What is gained out of being unkind?

Once you have done this look at the two. They will speak for themselves.

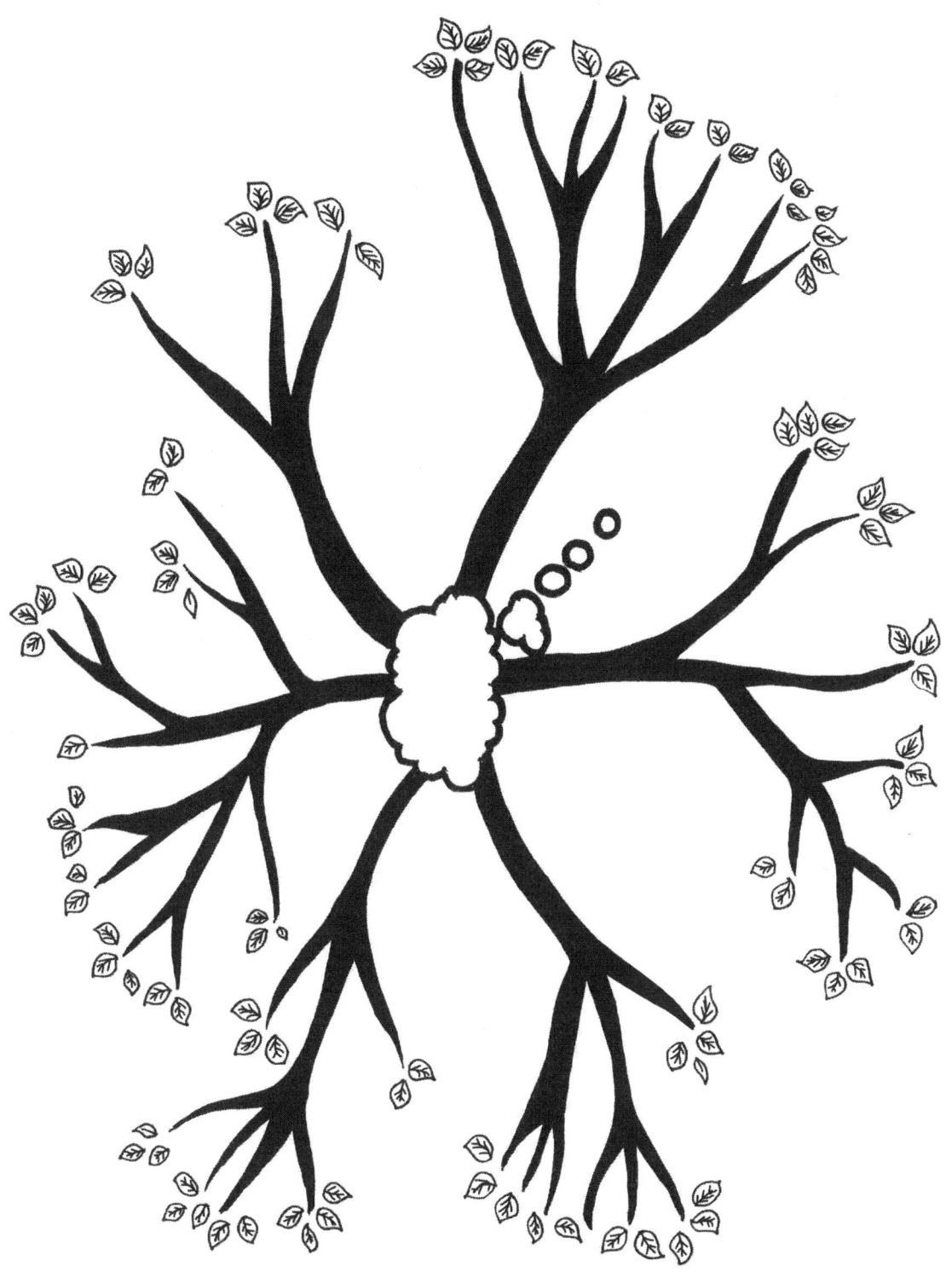

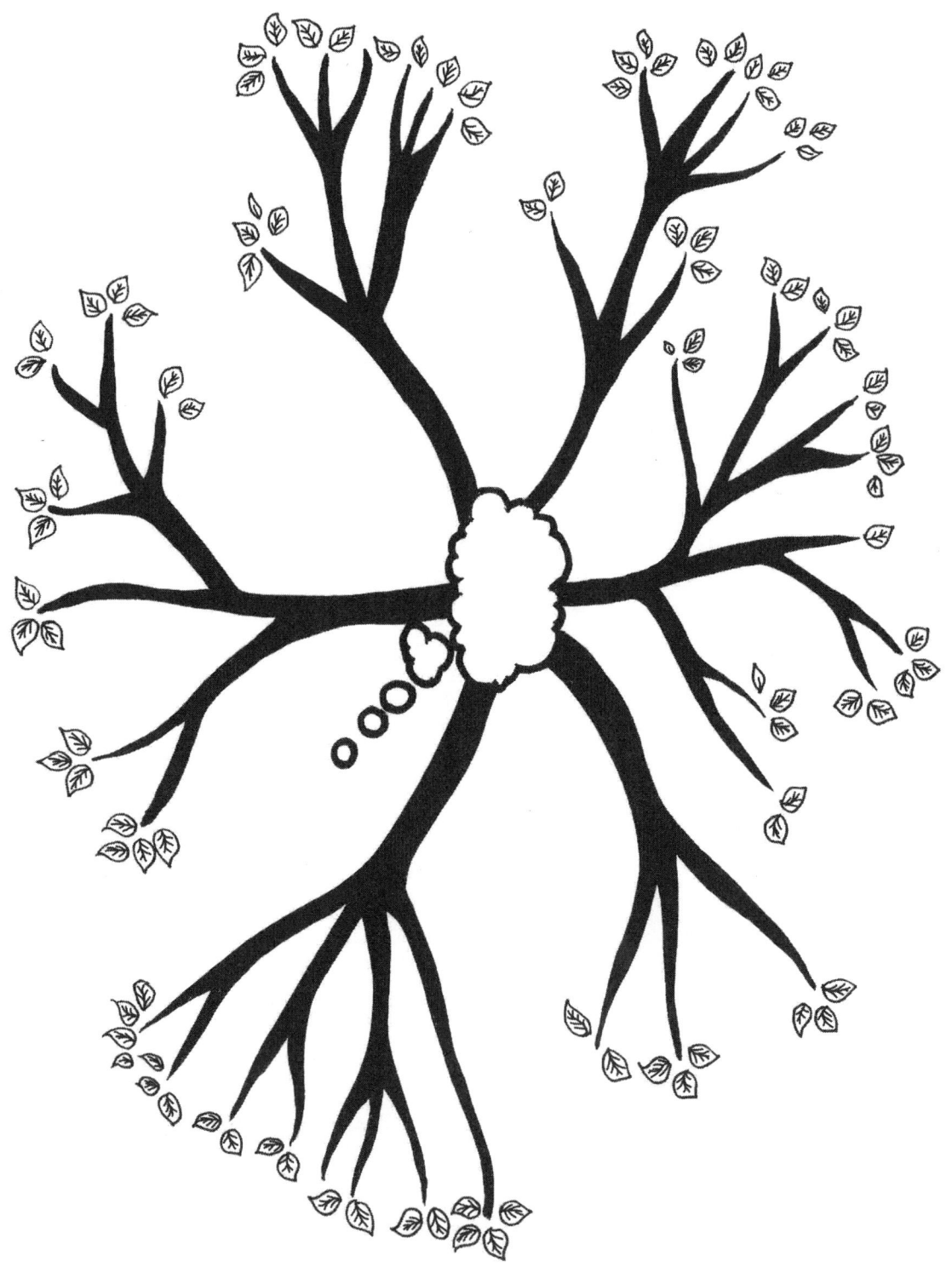

Now, write down all the things that others do for you that make you happy: the simple things, like when someone smiles at you, pays you a compliment, offers to carry your bag or notices your achievements. It could be Mum making you a cup of tea or giving your shoulders a massage. Get my drift?

_____

_____

_____

_____

_____

_____

_____

_____

_____

_____

_____

_____

Now find yourself an empty box, about 20cm by 20cm. You can even make one. Decorate it so that it's completely covered. Make it beautiful and name it your happiness box. Now, write down on individual pieces of paper all the things you came up with that bring you happiness. Decorate these pieces of paper and add them to your box. These will become part of the task for the week.

Random acts of kindness

Write down ten random acts of kindness you could do. They might even be something you do for a stranger. But make sure this is within a safe boundary. Check with an adult first.
Here are a few suggestions:

- Bake cookies for a lonely neighbour (ask an adult to deliver them)

- Send a card to your grandparents

- If age permits, babysit for a relative

You get it, right?
   Take time to write these acts of kindness down. Make the page creative.

These random acts of kindness can be completed over a long period. As you do them cross them off. Each time you do one write something about your experience. How did it feel? If it was something that gets a reaction, how did the person receiving the help respond?

10 Random acts of kindness

Notes

Task for the week

Each day for the coming week, blindly choose one of the pieces of paper from your happiness box. Whichever one you pick, carry out the act for someone. It doesn't have to be someone you know well; it could be the dinner lady or the school receptionist. Notice how you feel when you do something for someone else. Write about it on the page opposite.

Notes

A word from your mentor

You will feel good when you do something for others. Even a small thing like smiling at someone can brighten their day. You can't know how someone is feeling in that moment. A little act of kindness could be enough to change the way they are feeling, setting them up for a much better day.

Just by making these small adjustments to your life you will notice a difference in how you are feeling. Taking time to care for others is an important part of life. Doing kind things increases your self-confidence and self-worth. They make you feel purposeful. Also, when you put your attention on others it takes the attention away from yourself. It can be a good distraction, especially at times when you are feeling down.

"Ask yourself: Have you been kind today? Make kindness your daily modus operandi and change your world."
Annie Lennox

Week 9: Smartphone challenge

It is clear to me that the use of smartphones and other inventions has had a massive impact on girls, starting at a really young age. I have seen no end of problems arriving along with these gadgets. Of course, they can be useful, but like everything else in life there needs to be a balance. The problem is that it's easy to tune into our screens when we feel bored or low. They take us out of reality and provide a door to a whole new experience.

The question is, have you got your use of your smartphone under control? Time and time again I have witnessed how these devices are taking over lives. They are great when used positively, but when you use them to self evaluate or to constantly change the way you look in order to feel good, these devices can leave you feeling that you are never good enough. The survey below will help you to see how much you rely on your device. If you find that you are overusing your phone, you should start to find other ways to entertain yourself. You must always remember that there are so many other things you can do to fill your time: stuff that will make you feel good and give you back the inspiration and imagination that you may be lacking.

Have you ever considered that you might be addicted to using your phone?

What about how social media might be affecting you?

I am aware of the more serious problems that you might encounter from having a smartphone. Two of those things that come to the top of my list are sexting and grooming. These will be covered in week ten. For now let's focus on general everyday use.

following questions honestly. Write your answers below questions.

How many hours a day are you on your phone during the week?

___

How many hours on weekends or school holidays?

___

Do you look at it every time a message comes in?

___

Are all your notifications on?

___

Do you check it constantly to see how many likes you have?

___

If yes, what does it feel like if you see that you are not getting any?

___

Do you go to your phone first thing in the morning?

___

Do you go on your phone last thing at night?

___

Do you sleep with it by your bed?

___

Under your pillow?

___

Would you feel anxious if you didn't have it with you?

___

How many selfies do you take on an average day?

___

Do you Photoshop your image or change it in some way?

___

Do you feel social media has had a negative impact on your life? In what way?

___

Do you feel that you are spending too much time on your phone, at the expense of other activities?

Is social media affecting your confidence? If yes in what way?

On a scale of one to ten, what would you rate your phone usage in terms of how positive it makes you feel?

Fill in the chart on the next page: one side with all the positive things your smartphone can be used for, the other with all the dangers you can think of through smartphone use.

Task for the week

For the next week, I want you to choose to give something up on your phone. It can be as little as using it less, as much as deleting all your apps or anywhere in between. The braver you can be, the more positive changes in yourself are likely to be seen. I have not come across one girl who did not notice a positive change when trying this challenge for a week. At the end of the week, I want you to fill in the next page.

I would like you to write down any positive outcomes that you experienced: any little change in your mood or the way you feel about yourself or others around you. Every little detail counts. At the end of your challenge, I would ask you to share your outcome with someone you trust. It is good to share this experience because that person will give you feedback and this will encourage you to make other changes and to challenge your smartphone use. I want you to be aware of the difference, no matter how small. What is important here is that you experience the change.

Positive Changes

A word from your mentor

For some of you this exercise will be a breeze. You may find it easy to give up something. But for others it will not be so easy, and I am so proud of you for putting yourself to the test with this challenge. I am sure you will learn something from this. If the results are extremely positive, I would suggest that you consider making these changes permanent. You might see this as an opportunity to give up something that is not making you happy. Maybe until this point, you didn't realise how much all of this stuff was impacting you. Whatever happens next is up to you. But remember, it is exactly that: IT IS UP TO YOU!

You may want to consider the idea that if something is influencing your happiness and self esteem, isn't it time you made a change?

The thing is, your parents or carers probably have no idea what you are up to half the time, and they can't put a finger on the reasons that you are unhappy. They might have noticed that things started to change when you got access to a smartphone. But these things are here to stay, so it is up to you to manage its use. Your parents can lay down the rules, but it is so easy to break them when you can easily lie about just how much you are on your device or what it is you are up to. It is so important then that you take responsibility for your wellness and make sure the way you are using your device is safe and manageable. Talking to someone about this and allowing them to have access to what you are doing will help keep you safe. If the dangers are running high, you must try to understand that if you are keeping your parents out then they have no chance of protecting you. If you decide to shut them out, how can you expect them to keep you safe? Talking to your friends may not always be enough. Adults are far more mature and will know what to do to keep you safe. If necessary, PLEASE talk to someone you trust even if it is someone on the other end of a helpline.

Childline 0800 1111

"While you browse through images on Instagram, just remember that real life is in your heart, your smile, your family, your surroundings. Pictures online will make you believe you're not enough. Like you need to do something more… more exciting, be more physically beautiful, be more popular, be bigger than you are. You are real, you are beautiful, you are enough. Go and be in the world. Please don't compare yourself to the world's highlight reels and Photoshopped selfies."

Taken from www.weheartit.com

Week 10: Understanding sexting and grooming

Let's face it, this is an uncomfortable topic. But if you have not heard of these things, I feel the need to inform you. Some of you may be too young for this chapter, so if you think that's you, you can skip it. The thing is, what I see all too often in my work is that young girls are being drawn into harmful situations. So I feel it is my duty as your mentor to keep you safe and give you the tools you need to avoid this ever happening to you.

Girls as young as nine are being tricked and lied to online and sometimes are led into highly dangerous situations through no fault of their own; they simply don't understand the risk. Things can become really bad before the penny drops and a young girl recognises exactly what is going on. By this point she might have given away a lot of personal information. Some girls even meet up with strangers (people they thought they had made friends with) and sadly bad things have happened. I don't want to frighten you, but I feel you need to know. You need to be alert and wise up so that you do not become a victim of sexting or grooming.

What is sexting?

UKCCIS, the UK council for child internet safety, defines sexting in this way:

Whilst the term 'sexting' is often used by care professionals, there is no clear definition. Many professionals consider sexting to be 'sending or posting sexually suggestive images, including nude or semi-nude photographs, via mobiles or over the Internet. Yet when young people are asked 'What does sexting mean to you?' they are more likely to say something like 'sharing explicit messages with people they know'. Similarly, many parents think of sexting as flirty or sexual text messages rather than images.

Creating and sharing sexual photos and videos of under-18s is illegal. This makes dealing with such issues extremely complicated for schools and other agencies. It also presents a range of risks which need careful management.

The NSPCC defines grooming in this way:

Grooming is when someone builds a relationship, trust and emotional connection with a child or young person so they can manipulate, exploit and abuse them.

Children and young people who are groomed can be sexually abused, exploited or trafficked.

Anybody can be a groomer, no matter their age, gender or race. Grooming can take place over a short or long period of time—from weeks to years. Groomers may also build a relationship with the young person's family or friends to make them seem trustworthy or authoritative. Taken from NSPCC website: www.nspcc.org.uk

The crucial question every young girl should be able to answer is whether someone in their life has crossed a boundary. Sexting and grooming lead to serious problems, but the trouble creeps up gradually. What is harmless chat and what is not okay? That line is easy to miss, and you need to be so sharp to make sure it isn't crossed.

The worst part is that you are probably enjoying the attention, and you don't want to lose that. Be honest: we all like getting attention from people, don't we? So you push the boundaries a little at a time because what's the harm? Well, maybe there is no harm until suddenly there is.

Please understand that line is *so* important. Your self-respect is one of the most important things you have. Young girls have watched their lives spiral down into a terrible place. Once you're down there, you can always climb back up but it is so much harder than spotting that line right at the moment when you cross it. So, respect yourself. Be sharp. Value your dignity more than flattering comments from some person. I know you can do it, but I just want you to pay attention. If you are like most girls, your online life is probably pretty hidden from adult eyes, so once again this one is on you. Your life, your happiness.

Questionnaire

It's all about not crossing that line, and no one but you can say exactly where that line is. I can't do that for you. What I can do is help you to be more aware. When you learn to pay attention instead of just not thinking about it, you will find you have no trouble knowing when things go too far. It's an instinct, and everyone has it as long as they stay watchful.

The questions below don't have right or wrong answers, but they will push you to look at things properly and be honest with yourself. You do not have to write the answers down. This one you can keep private. But answer them honestly to yourself.

- Has anyone asked you for, or sent you, sexy photos? Nude photos clearly cross a line, but has someone asked you just to show a bit more skin? Maybe in your underwear? They may ask this in a friendly way, to build your trust. They may show you their body first. But it is not normal to ask you to do this.

- Have you sent these kinds of pictures? Have you been tempted to?

- Has anyone ever talked to you about what you look like under your clothes?

- Have you found yourself in a group on your phone, but then someone has singled you out for a private chat? The group may or may not include people you know in the real world, but suddenly you are chatting privately with a stranger. Have you been asked about personal things, like where you live or go to school? Remember, you have absolutely no idea who you are talking to. It might be someone you would automatically avoid if they approached you in the street, but online they can just pretend to be a young person just like you.

- Has anyone ever secretly befriended you and started to tell you that you are fun and pretty? Has anyone encouraged you to spend more time online or in person with them?

- Do you have a friend you keep secret, maybe someone older than you? Has anyone asked you not to mention them to others? Ask yourself this: why would you keep a friend secret? It's a huge warning sign if you are friends with someone you don't want your regular friends to know about.

- Is someone talking to you about sex and making sexual jokes?

- Is anyone asking you to do anything you are uncomfortable with?

- Is someone new in your life offering to buy you gifts? This is another huge warning sign, *especially* if they're offering this in exchange for something.

- Has anyone touched you somewhere you did not want them to? Have you ever let someone touch you in a way that you later regretted?

- Has anything else like these things happened, anything which you felt was not right?

If you have answered 'no' to all the above questions, I am sorry that you had to go through this questionnaire but the sad fact is that this stuff happens and it can happen to girls who are otherwise absolutely fine. It can sneak up on anyone. I ask you to be mindful of these things in the future and remember to come back to these questions if you ever feel the need. For now you can skip to the next chapter. The task for the week is only for girls who had a 'yes'.

If you did answer yes to any of the questions then I set you this next task in the hope that you will see it through. If there is only one task in this book that you actually follow, *please* make it this one.

Task for the week

The task is simple: you need to tell someone what happened.

Maybe you already did something that you know you should not have done, or maybe you feel there's not much to tell. Maybe you just had a feeling inside that a line was crossed. Maybe you are tempted to do something you think you might later regret.

Let's be honest, it's super awkward to talk about these kinds of things. You probably really don't want to. You would probably rather deal with it by yourself. It'll be all right. I can handle it. Please, don't risk it.

Whatever it was that you answered yes to, someone who loves you really wants to know about it. They want to help you to understand things from a different perspective. You might think older people are not very cool (and you might be right!) but the thing is they have seen a thing or two, and they've probably figured out a few things. Think about how much more clued up you are now than you were just one year ago. A lot, right? If you are worried that you might be crossing the line we have talked about, you need that perspective from someone older. The obvious person would be your mum, dad or carer, but if for whatever reason that doesn't work for you, talk to someone responsible like your favourite teacher. If there's no one at school you feel comfortable with, then call the helpline I've given below.

Please reach out, no matter how small or how normal you feel the situation is. Remember things start small and gradually change. You might feel ashamed, but I promise this feeling will start to go away as soon as you have shared it with someone. You must speak out. You might be worried that it's going to get blown up into a big deal, but that's because people are concerned about your well-being. You could be getting yourself into a lot of danger. I have said it before: there are people in this world who care about you and your well-being. They will be able to give you the best advice. They are here to help you.

Childline: 0800 1111

A word from your mentor

Please always remember that whenever you post something online, this post can be kept by another person forever. It can even be posted online and shared by people you've never met. You may think you know all the people you are sharing things with, but this is not always the case. Most of the social media apps have groups, and these groups often become really big. You won't know everyone in the group, but they've all got full access to everything you post. You may add yourself to a group that looks fun. You might join a large group without being aware of it. You could then find yourself being singled out by someone you feel is a friend just because they were in the same group as you and your friends.

A social media group that seems harmless in the beginning can quickly start to turn sexual. It might just feel like a bit of fun. In that moment, before you post an image, you need to tell yourself: once this image leaves my hands there's no taking it back. It could be halfway around the world. There could be a thousand copies. It could show up in ten years. It might even be found by a potential employer one day, looking you up online.

At your age falling in and out of relationships with boys and girls can be another source of big problems. Promises to keep things private can be broken. People do crazy things when they are hurt. Just because you trust someone now doesn't make it safe to share private things with them. The only way to really protect your privacy is not to post in the first place.

If, on the other hand, you find yourself being the one encouraging this kind of stuff, please ask yourself if you have thought of the bigger picture and how this could backfire on you. There are legalities involved in sexting, and if you are caught sharing or receiving sexual content there is every chance you could be prosecuted.

On the grooming side, the scary part is that these predators know what they are doing. They know the typical weaknesses of young girls and how to exploit them. They know how to get under your skin. They might convince you they are the best friend you ever had, even that they love you and want to be your boyfriend. So many girls have fallen for it. Before the idea of meeting them ever comes up, they will try to have you so convinced that you even go against the people you love. Predators know how to set themselves up as young people, and sometimes they can be very young too.

In one way these people are clever, but they're also stupid. It's absolutely easy to stay out of their way if you just know how to pay attention, and most of all if you respect yourself and don't let yourself get sucked in by pretty words. Stand on your own two feet. You don't need some random guy on the Internet to tell you how great you are. I can do that and I haven't even met you. You are great! But the point is, YOU need to tell YOURSELF that you are great. Because it's true. Stand up straight, stick your chin out and just be you. None of these problems will be able to touch you then.

STAY SAFE, BE BRAVE.
YOU ARE WORTH SO MUCH.

Remember these SMART rules to keep you safe.

S: Stay safe, don't give out your personal information to people you don't know.

M: Don't meet up with anyone you have only been in touch with online. Always check with a trusted adult.

A: Accepting pictures, texts or files from someone you don't know can lead to problems.

R: Reliable. Check all information before you believe it. Ask yourself, is the person or the website telling the truth?

T: Tell an adult if someone or something makes you feel concerned, scared or uncomfortable.

Week 11: Taking care of me

When was the last time you did something just for you? Are you taking time to take care of yourself and be kind to yourself? It is important to take time out of your everyday life for the things that are good for your well-being. We so often get bogged down in life and forget to do the things that we love and enjoy. So why not make these part of your routine? We all need balance, and part of that balance is the things that are just for us.

It could be a walk in the woods or spending time with someone you love. You may find that for you it's all about being creative—cooking, painting, or reading a good book. Whatever it is that you enjoy, you must find time for it.

If you think about all the things you spend your time on, and ask yourself whether you find those things uplifting or not, where would the answers take you? You might realise that you need to rethink where you give your time. If you make little changes to fit in the activities you love, you may find you have more motivation and more energy for all the other necessary things in life.

Take a look at the self care wheel on this page. Read it over and get a feel for the things that stand out for you. On the blank wheel, I would like you to fill in the empty spaces. Write down all the things that you feel you need right now. Maybe there are things you have not done for a long time. If you had the ideal self care wheel, what would it look like? Be sure to choose activities which lift your mood and energise you.

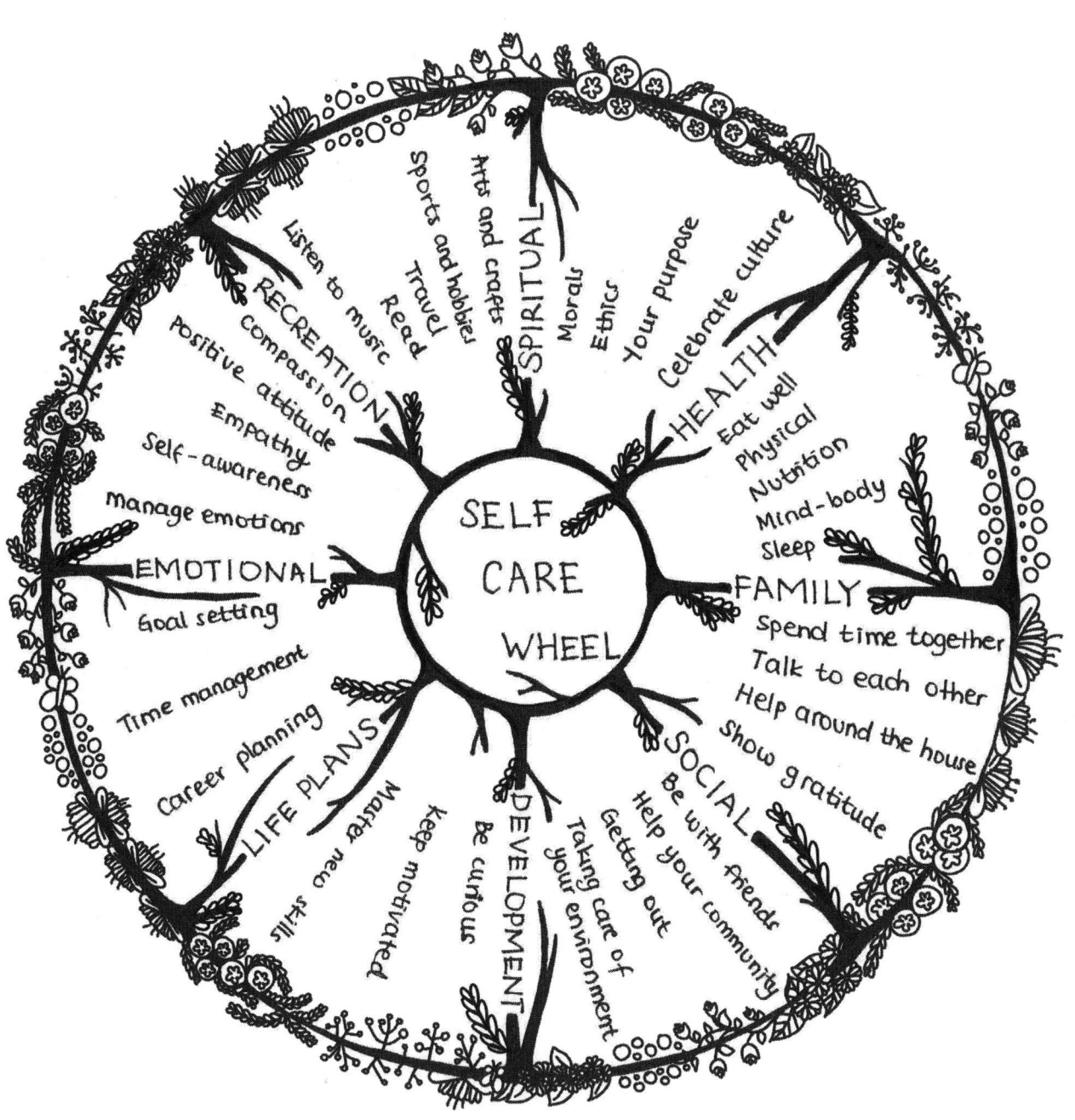

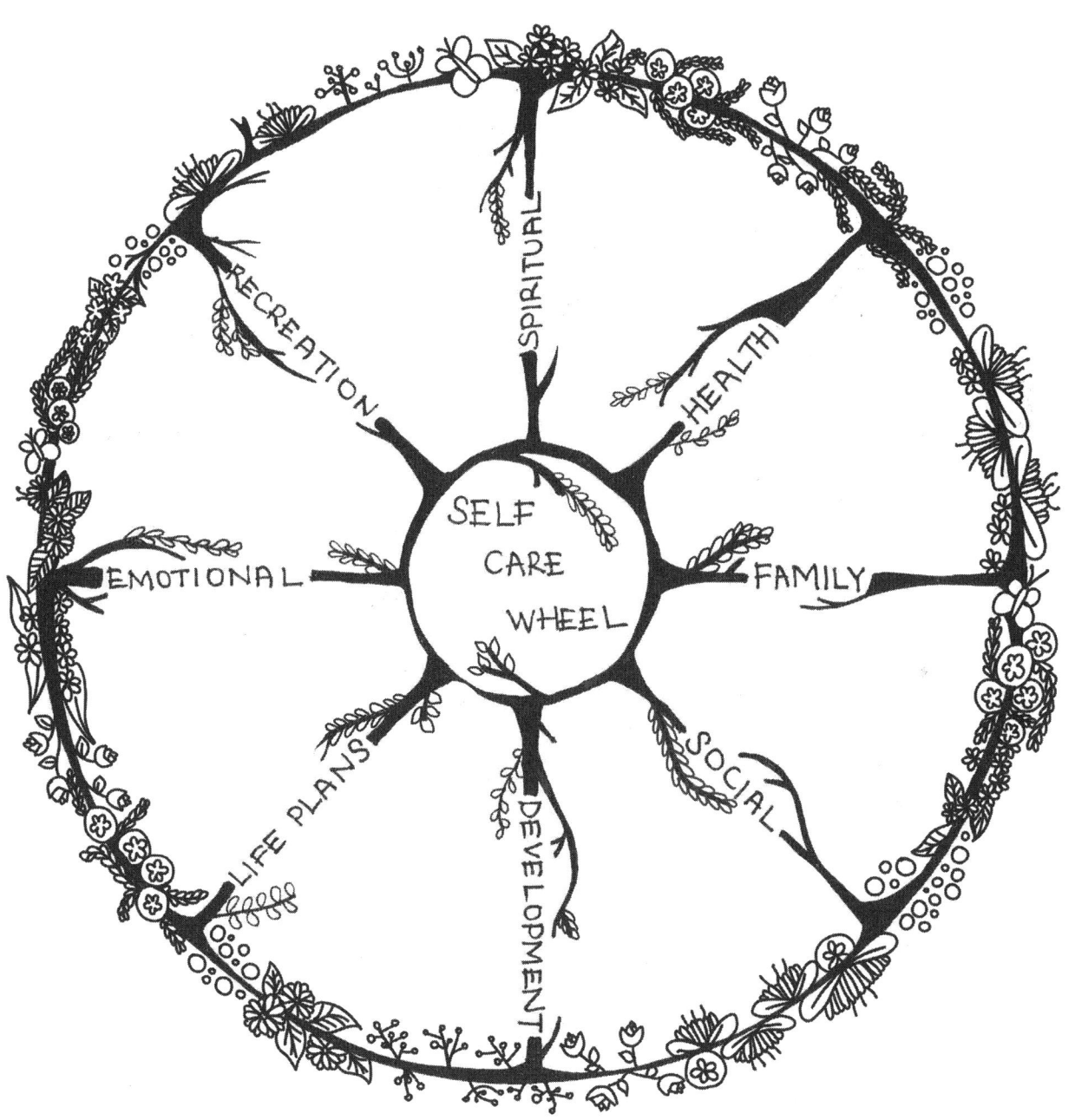

Task for the week

Take something from your self care wheel and make it happen. Try to do more than one in a week. While you are doing this task, reflect on how you are feeling. Make a note of your feelings on the blank page. If the page gets filled, use your own paper and clip it into your journal. Write down what effect it has on you when you take the time to take care of your needs. Experiment with different choices so that you can start to see what really works for you. Once you know which activities lift you up, you should aim to make them part of your daily or weekly routine. This will have such a positive effect on you.

Notes

A word from your mentor

I would not hold back on anything here. Go all out to indulge yourself. You might go for a swim or to the gym. You might have a hot bath with scented salts (good for the muscles). Whatever it is, take your time to enjoy yourself and relax. Notice how it makes you feel. Doing things that lift or soothe your mood will help bring you into a positive state. There is a lot of science to back up how important these things are. Just five minutes of meditation, for example, can reduce your stress levels and help you to feel good about yourself. Relaxing breathing techniques practised for just a few mins each day can impact how you well you sleep at night and improve your levels of stress and anxiety. Dancing and singing can boost your mood and make you feel happy. It is important to make habits of these positive things. They won't take up much of your time and in fact could lead to a much more productive day or week. You will be amazed at how much difference these little changes make. Take care of yourself! Put your well-being first. You may not see it now, but everything you do will impact your well-being in the future. It's good to see this as making an investment in yourself, an investment in your future.

Week 12: Inspirational people, powerful me!

As a young girl, it is important for you to believe in yourself. At this stage in life, you might be thinking of what you want to become. Keep your options open. Think big and imagine all those things you could be. You have every right to follow your dreams. Thinking about what inspires you will help you to discover where your values lie and what it is that makes you come alive inside.

A great way to help explore these questions about yourself and your future is to get inspired by others. Who is it that motivates you? Who is it that impresses you and why? Who do you aspire to be like?

If someone stands out to you then follow your heart and tap into what it is about them that brings you to life. Is it what they have achieved? What they do for others? What is it that triggers your imagination and keeps you going? Don't just follow famous people, or follow people for their looks. Think about the people around you. It could even be a member of your family who stands out. It could be someone who is kind and helps others or animals.

A good way to pull together all the people who inspire you is to make a collage. You can use a piece of cardboard to do this. Cut out pictures from magazines, use photographs or print pictures from the Internet. You can choose both real people and fictional characters. Use powerful words to describe what you feel about the impact these people have had on your life. Cut out words or write them yourself and use them in your collage. Why do these people stand out in your world? What have they done to inspire you? Write it down. Imagine that one day you will also become someone who will inspire others. Think about what that means for you. What is it that you would like to do in your life?

On the next page, I want you to write ten powerful affirmations starting with I AM.
    For example, tell yourself

I AM… going to achieve all the things I want

I AM… beautiful inside and out

I AM… brave and bold

I AM… going to be an author of great books

Make them bold and powerful statements, things you would not normally believe about yourself.

I am...

1. I am...

2. I am...

3. I am...

4. I am...

5. I am...

6. I am...

7. I am...

8. I am...

9. I am...

10. I am...

Task for the week

Now that you have chosen your affirmations, I want you to say them every day. You can even say them to yourself when you're looking in the mirror. If you like, you can shout them out as loudly as you can. You might feel you don't really believe some of these things, but here's the trick: it doesn't matter. Just say them anyway. Don't think about it, don't question them, just say them. It has an effect. It really works. It will start to change your beliefs about yourself. Notice how you feel when you say them. At first you might feel self-conscious, but keep going. When you lie in bed at night, try saying them to yourself before you fall asleep. Let them sink into your head.

A word from your mentor

It is sometimes hard for us to believe in ourselves. This is a normal trait that many girls share. Even the ones out there who seem to have it all. Make no mistake, life is probably not always so easy for them either. I bet they also had the same difficulties that you may find yourself in. We often put ourselves down and feel we are not capable of certain things in life. But who told you that? Did you tell it to yourself? If you did, you had no right. If you tell yourself something over and over again you will start to believe it. Look back at your collage of all the people who have inspired you. Remind yourself that they too have probably had the same negative thoughts as you. We all battle with our thoughts. We all have negative beliefs about ourselves. But these are just stories we tell ourselves. We all create our own story. Once you know that, you also know that you can change your story.

On the next couple of pages are just three of the young girls who have changed the world.

Greta Thunberg

Born in 2003, this Swedish teen activist has become a leading voice for climate change activism.

"If you still say that we are wasting valuable lesson time, then let me remind you that our political leaders have wasted decades through denial and inaction."
Greta Thunberg

Malala Yousafzai

When she was 11, Malala Yousafzai wrote and published an anonymous diary about her life in Pakistan under Taliban rule which quickly gained huge attention. Soon she began to speak out more publicly about the need for girls to have proper access to education.

But three years later her life changed forever when, in retaliation for her activism, she was shot in the head by a gunman on a school bus.

The assassination attempt didn't stop her, however, and her profile has only risen further since then. She has appeared on the front cover of Time magazine, and in 2014 she became the youngest person ever to win the Nobel Peace Prize.

"This award is not just for me. It is for those forgotten children who want education."
Malala Yousafzai

Emma González

Emma is a survivor of an American high school shooting who has become an activist and advocate for gun control. In March 2018, she delivered a powerful speech at the March for our Lives in Washington DC, when she read out the names of her dead classmates and then stood defiantly silent for four minutes—the length of time it took the gunman to carry out his attack.

> *"If the president wants to come up to me and tell me to my face that it was a terrible tragedy and… how nothing is going to be done about it, I'm going to happily ask him how much money he received from the National Rifle Association."*
> Emma González

Week 13: Stress, anxiety and depression

This week we will take a close look at these all too common difficulties and see if they are present in your life in some way. All the things we have covered in this book so far (if taken seriously) can help lead you to happiness and well-being. I believe that if you use the tools in this book you can prevent yourself from becoming seriously unwell or unhappy. These days there is a lot of focus on therapy and counselling to deal with these kinds of problems, but it is my firm belief that *prevention* is the key to good health and well-being. There is lots of wisdom in the old saying that an ounce of prevention is worth a pound of cure. Maybe for you modern girls we need to say a few grams of prevention is worth a kilo of cure!

This book has already given you many tools to work with. I hope that by the time you get to this part of the book, you will have already gained an insight into how you can feel better by using these tools. However, I am aware that for some of you the levels at which you experience stress or anxiety will be the main factor in how happy you are. If these things are left too long, they can become hard to combat. But no matter how bad it has got for you, you must know that there are solutions to these problems. Let's get a better understanding of them.

Stress

Stress is the body's way of responding to threat. This can be anything from a deadline at school to being late for an appointment. Usually, a person quickly gets over this and moves on. If you feel like there is too much stress in your life, you can find ways to manage it, such as the breathing and meditation the exercise we saw in Week 1. Other things like good sleep and exercise improve stress. These tools can keep you in good health and should be used regularly, and especially any time you find yourself dealing with increased levels of stress, such as at the time of exams. Using these exercises regularly will prevent you from becoming overstressed and can calm you down when stress tries to trip you up.

Anxiety

If you do not keep on top of your stress it can lead to anxiety. Anxiety is different from stress because it stays longer in the body and can leave you feeling tired or emotionally drained. Anxiety is more complicated than stress. It can make you feel more uptight and can lead you to worrying and overthinking. Anxiety can develop into stronger fears, and eventually into anxiety attacks or panic attacks (people use both terms but they are really the same thing). These attacks can come when we sort of think ourselves into more and more extreme worries and fears. The thoughts can become exaggerated and build up a story in our mind which is more and more disconnected from reality but feels totally real when we are in it. On a physical level, girls have reported to me that they feel their heart is racing, they feel hot and even start sweating. These feelings can in themselves be frightening. Some girls report the experience of tummy aches or dizziness. Others have said that panic attacks can make their chest feel tight and make them feel like it's difficult to breathe. These feelings normally pass quite quickly. It is not always easy in that moment. Of course, you should always talk to a doctor whenever you have symptoms that don't go away.

Your thoughts can be overwhelming, but remember: thoughts are not facts. Negative thoughts can develop into a story we tell ourselves, as we discussed in Week 7. The thought chart from that week can be really useful if you are feeling anxious. Ask yourself: are these thoughts true? Do you have any real evidence? What could you change the thought to? What can you do from all the previous exercises that will help you to let go of negative thoughts?

At any sign of anxiety or panic, the breathing exercises from Week 1 are the best thing to try first. If you can be strong enough to focus your attention on your breathing, your anxiety or panic should subside and your heart rate return to normal. But I understand that when you are in the moment, unless you have someone to talk you through it, you may find it difficult to calm down. If you know you are prone to these problems, it's a good idea to talk about the various solutions with someone else, if possible a family member so that they will know what to do when the time comes. That way it won't feel so scary and you will have help. Don't feel ashamed. Show them your star from Week 1 and explain to them what you would like them to do if they see you getting panicky. Many people suffer from anxiety attacks and panic attacks and – rest assured – by talking with someone you will feel so much better.

If the breathing exercises are not enough to calm you down, telling someone is important because they can help you work out what is the best thing to do. They may take you to the doctor. It is better to get it out in the open and get on top of it. Knowing what to do in a moment of panic will help you to feel you have control. And always bear in mind it might be worth seeing a counsellor for a while. There is nothing like having someone to support you and help you through, until everything gets a bit more under control. Having a better understanding will take away the fear.

Depression

"I have found that with depression, one of the most important things you could realise is that you're not alone."
Dwayne Johnson

Sadly, young people also suffer from depression. Symptoms range from lasting feelings of unhappiness and hopelessness to losing interest in the things you used to enjoy, and feeling tearful. Like everything, in small doses this is okay, but if you feel this seems to be going on for weeks or even months then you need to talk to someone. You may even find yourself having suicidal thoughts. These thoughts can come when you feel like life is not worth living or if you feel that you are not worthy of existing.

Please rest assured that this can happen to anyone. You are not alone, and professional counsellors are highly experienced with these things. They can help you to untangle the thoughts and feelings and get you back to a place that feels positive and happy. I suffered from depression when I was young, so I know exactly how this feels. It can feel scary and it can also feel like it will never go away. When you are deep in this way of thinking, it can be hard to imagine that life could be better. It can leave you feeling that the people around you would be better off without you, but this is not true. If anything happened to you, your family and friends would be devastated. No matter how dark your thoughts are, I want you to know that this can change and you can be happy again. PLEASE seek help if your thoughts about yourself are constantly making you feel this way.

Self harm

Self harm is when somebody purposely hurts or injures their body, such as by cutting themselves. It's usually a way of coping with or releasing strong emotional distress and sadly has become common among young people. If something difficult is going on inside you, and you don't know how to let the emotions out, self harm can feel like a kind of self control. It is something young people might turn to if they feel they have no other way of dealing with prolonged feelings of anxiousness, depression, or being bullied.

As with all the advice in this chapter, if you find yourself in this place, the most important advice I can possibly give is *please get help*. Please share your troubles with someone. It is too much to deal with by yourself. If, for whatever reason, there is no one around you feel you can turn to then please use one of the helplines given below:

Childline (24 hours)
Freephone: 0800 1111
    Contact www.childline.org.uk

Young Minds Crisis Messenger
Provides 24/7 crisis support. If you need urgent help text YM to 85258. All texts are answered by trained volunteers, with support from experienced clinical supervisors.

Calm Harm App

www.calmharm.co.uk, a free app providing support and strategies to help you resist or manage the urge to self harm.

Questionnaire

The questionnaire below, taken from the NHS, covers all of the above topics. It will help you to identify your level of stress, anxiety or depression.

Give yourself a score from zero to five for each of the behaviours with zero being "not at all" and five being "a lot". If you find yourself measuring two or above you should talk them over with an adult you feel safe with. It might be hard to measure exactly what you are feeling just by answering the questions below, which is why it is so important to talk them through with someone who can help you get a better understanding of your health and well-being.

If you answer four or five on any of these, and you don't want to talk to a family member, I urge you not to leave it. Please don't use any excuses to put it off. Call Childline on the number below. It can also be a lot easier to talk to someone you don't know, and it can really help:

Childline freephone 0800 1111

On a scale of zero to five, do you experience…

Obsessive worrying:	1	2	3	4	5
Fear that things will go wrong:	1	2	3	4	5
Social shyness and embarrassment:	1	2	3	4	5
Feeling tense and on edge:	1	2	3	4	5
Obsessive behaviours:	1	2	3	4	5
Hair pulling, skin picking:	1	2	3	4	5
Cutting yourself:	1	2	3	4	5
Clinginess:	1	2	3	4	5
Difficulties concentrating:	1	2	3	4	5
Irritability and angry outbursts:	1	2	3	4	5
Dizziness and feeling light-headed:	1	2	3	4	5
Hot and cold flushes:	1	2	3	4	5
Stomach complaints, nausea and vomiting:	1	2	3	4	5

Headaches:	1	2	3	4	5
Difficulties sleeping:	1	2	3	4	5
Tiredness when it's not late:	1	2	3	4	5
Loss of appetite:	1	2	3	4	5
The need to hide away:	1	2	3	4	5
Feeling sad:	1	2	3	4	5
Feeling hopeless and helpless:	1	2	3	4	5
Low self-esteem:	1	2	3	4	5
Feeling tearful:	1	2	3	4	5
Feeling guilt-ridden:	1	2	3	4	5
Feeling irritable and intolerant of others:	1	2	3	4	5
Lack of motivation or interest in things:	1	2	3	4	5
Finding it difficult to make decisions:	1	2	3	4	5

Not getting any enjoyment out of life: 1 2 3 4 5

Thoughts of suicide or self harm: 1 2 3 4 5

Avoiding contact with friends: 1 2 3 4 5

Neglecting your hobbies and interests: 1 2 3 4 5

Difficulties in your home, or family life: 1 2 3 4 5

Task for the week

Another stress buster

Find a quiet spot and lie down. This is a muscle loosening exercise. It will help you to fully relax your whole body. It's a good idea to play some quiet music. Nature music is instrumental music with the sounds of nature. You can find it on Spotify, or other music media. Look up instrumental nature music. It is very soothing. Often people listen to the sounds of nature when going to sleep. It is a great way to help those of us who struggle to nod off.

Close your eyes and focus on your breathing. Remember the deep breathing in Week 1? If you haven't made this a daily habit, then I suggest you do. Remember to breathe deeply. You can put both your hands on your tummy. Feel it lift up and then release all the old air out into the atmosphere. Breathe it all out and then slowly fill your lungs with new, fresh air. Don't go too fast or you might feel a bit dizzy. When you start to feel more relaxed, take your attention away from the breathing. I want you to pay attention to your body. Clench your toes. Now release them and let them relax into the space. Go slowly and repeat the same for the back of your calves, your thighs, your buttocks, your arms, your chest then your shoulders. Do this slowly, and each time notice how relaxed your body is becoming as you let it sink into the space. Lie there in this moment and enjoy the calm peace.

Stay as long as you like. When you are ready, slowly sit up. Wait a moment before you get up. Take a look at the room around you and make contact with the objects in the room. This will help you to feel grounded.

You can carry out this exercise last thing at night. It will help prepare you for a good night's sleep.

A word from your mentor

I hope this week has helped you to question the level at which you suffer stress, anxiety, depression, panic attacks, or self harm. A certain amount of stress or anxiety can be quite normal, but you need to know when you have crossed the line. If these things persist, you need to seek help and talk to someone. You have to be honest with yourself if you reach the point where it is becoming a bigger problem. If you can keep an eye on this you will find it much easier to cope when difficult situations come about.

I can't stress enough how critical it is to look after your well-being. Finding ways to release stress will prevent these things from building up. When you notice your levels of stress and anxiety rising, do something about it. All these things are warning signs. If you touch something burning hot, it hurts because your body wants to teach you not to do it. All these mental health issues are the same. Your body is telling you something is wrong, but unlike the burn, the source of the problem can be far less obvious. That is why you need someone else's help, to connect the dots. Listen to what your body is telling you. It wants you to be well. Don't miss the signs.

There is lots of help available. There are people who care about you, and there are helplines you can call. The important point is to remember that these problems can be solved. And remember that you are worth it. Your existence on this earth is **VERY IMPORTANT**. You are very much needed, and what you learn from these difficulties will help you to become stronger and more compassionate towards others. The world needs young girls like you. What you go through in life can lead you to help others.

Week 14: Healthy eating, sleeping and exercise!

At your age and stage in life, you must make sure you eat well. Your body is growing and changing all the time. Your brain will keep growing until you are in your early twenties so you must feed it well. Food will also affect your mood. It is well known that having a good diet will keep you from feeling tired and sluggish both in mind and body. It is equally important that you don't make food a big issue, for example worrying about how much and what you eat for fear of gaining weight.

We all have different bodies; humans come in different shapes and sizes. This is normal. It makes us who we are. If you were to imagine a world where everyone was the same, it would be pretty weird, right?

You should be proud of your body. Thank it for being there for you, for getting you to the places you need to go, for allowing you to exist. Loving and accepting who you are is important. We all come with our imperfections, but it is those imperfections that make us who we are.

Unfortunately, many girls go through life struggling to love and enjoy their body. The media sets you up to believe it is vital to be slim and conform to a certain look. Smartphones and social media do not help. You are constantly being told lies about how you should look and that if you don't fit the mould then you are ugly. All this pressure makes girls unhappy. The fashion industry is fuelled by this unhappiness. The more you worry about your imperfections, the more you pollute our mind with a negative story about yourself. It's time to wake up and stop playing their game.

Many young girls just like you end up with serious health issues around body dissatisfaction. It can be anything from hating their bodies to more serious conditions like anorexia nervosa and bulimia. I am not an expert in eating disorders, so once again my advice is to encourage you to get proper help if you feel you are having trouble with eating in any way. Take it seriously. Big problems always start small, so don't put it off! If you are secretly bingeing and then throwing up your food or throwing away food without eating it, please tell someone. What I do know about eating disorders is they can become highly dangerous. So please, if you find yourself obsessing over your weight or behaving unusually around food, please get help.

Beat eating disorder's helpline:
0808 801 0711

Open 365 days a year, 12–8pm Monday to Friday and 4–8pm on weekends and bank holidays.

www.beateatingdisorders.org.uk

Let's take a look at what is a balanced way of eating.

According to the NHS, this chart below is what a healthy diet looks like. Take a look at it. Compared to the chart, ask yourself how well you are doing. Do you feel you have a healthy diet?

Now, using the empty chart below, fill in the blanks with your own diet. If you have a poor diet full of sugary drinks and lots of cakes and biscuits it is likely that this will not only impact on your weight but it will might also affect your mental heath.

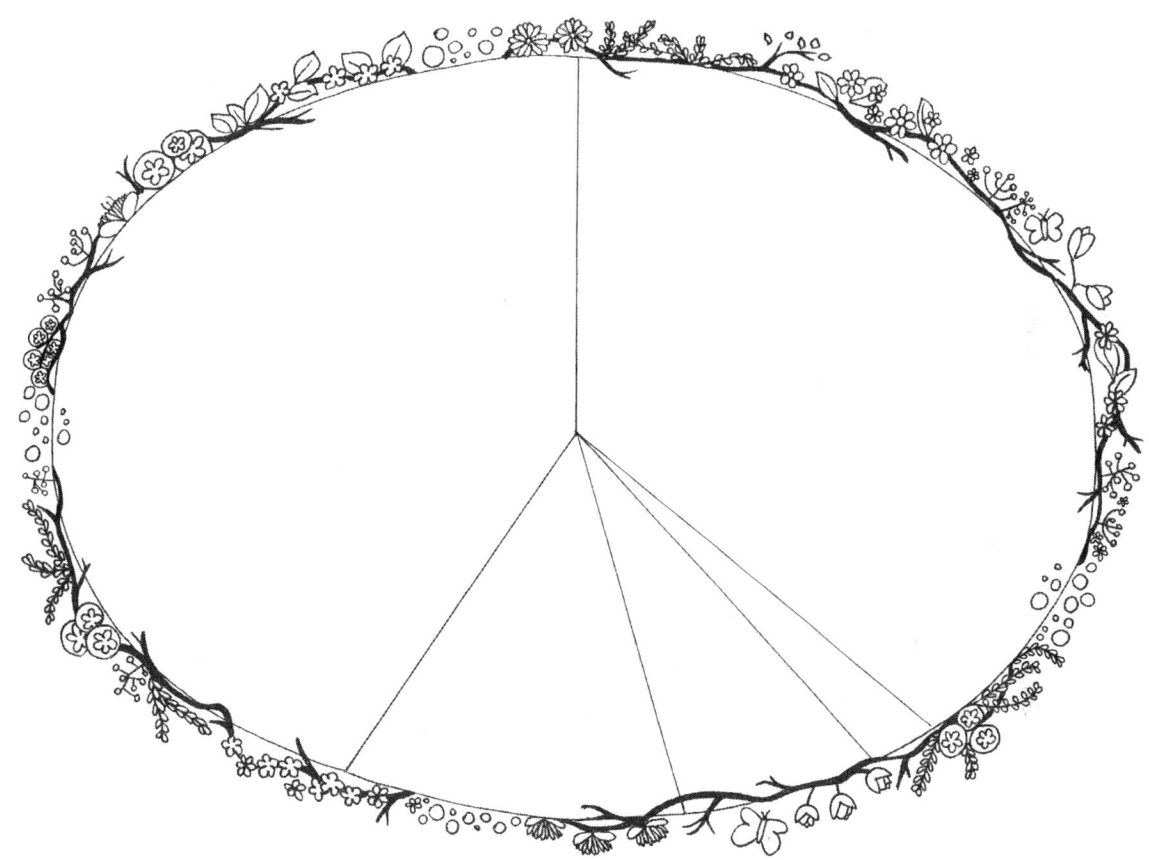

Having looked at the NHS food chart, do you feel your diet is healthy and well balanced? If your menu is balanced it should look a lot like this one. Of course, you don't have to be eating everything on this chart. It's just a guide. If you are vegetarian or vegan, you won't see any meat or dairy on your chart, but you must make sure you are getting a good amount of protein from other foods.

Exercise also plays a big role in your well-being. If you are exercising enough, you will find that your body is in good shape. If you are not exercising enough, then you may want to try to find an exercise that you enjoy. It can be anything from a sport to a dance class, yoga or the gym. Any kind of exercise will help you in so many ways. It will allow you to release stress, and it will keep your body fit and alive.

If you find yourself in front of a screen too often, try to take more time doing something that gets your body moving. If you have a dog, taking him or her out for a walk could be all you need. Getting outside and into nature is really relaxing, and if you go with someone else it's a great opportunity for a chat and a catch up.

A quick word on sleep. Sleep is extremely important for you at your age. It should be regular, and you should make sure you get enough of it. Try to come off any screens an hour before you go to bed. This will help you to fall asleep quicker and will allow your mind to rest well before sleep. If you have difficulties sleeping then I urge you to think about what it is that could be causing you to sleep badly. The main culprits are late nights and screens. They are both highly addictive, and you might want to put in boundaries that help you. Asking a parent to take away your devices an hour before going to bed is a good start. If you have no devices in your bedroom, there is no temptation. See this as an act of kindness to yourself, something that plays a role in your well-being and happiness.

If you are not doing any exercise, use the page opposite to write down all the practical things you could do to get more exercise. Try to add things that you can get started on right away. If it's a class that you want to take, that's fine, but also add a few things that can be done right now. A ten-minute walk every day is good enough if that's all you can manage. Maybe you could walk to school instead of getting a lift.

Here are a few suggestions:

- Walking

- Cycling

- Sport

- Dance

- Table tennis or badminton

- Swimming

Practical things I could do to get more exercise:

Task for the week

Take another look at your food chart to see if it measures well against the NHS food chart. If you are lacking in something, I want you to choose something from the NHS chart and add it to your diet. Over the coming days, add new things to your diet and see if you can make your chart balance up, the same way the NHS one does. Make a list of the things you lack, and talk to a parent or carer about how you could add them to your diet. If you find you binge on chocolates, sweets, crisps or cakes regularly, try to cut back. If you cut back on these things, you will notice a difference not just to your body but to your mind and to your emotions too.

Next, if you are not one for exercise, I would like you to pick something that is realistic and practical from your list and include it in the week ahead. Make sure you don't put it off by deciding you need to wait and get yourself booked on to a class or anything like that. Start today!

A note from your mentor

As you improve your diet and start to get some exercise, write down any changes you notice. It is important to make a note of these changes so that you can measure your progress and start to learn what works for you. Treat it as an experiment.

If you find you are having any tummy complaints, keeping a food diary is one way to see get on top of it. Each day record what you have eaten and how your day has gone, both physically and emotionally. After a while, you will start to see a pattern.

Most importantly, love your body, be kind to it, stop trying to be like everyone else. You are unique, and that is what makes you special.

Here are ten steps to positive body image from the National Eating Disorders Association. www.nationaleatingdisorders.org You will find that some of these steps are in this book. Use them wisely.

1. Appreciate all your body can do.

2. Keep a top ten list of things you like about yourself, things that aren't related to how much you weigh or what you look like.

3. Remind yourself that 'true beauty' is not simply skin deep. Beauty is a state of mind, not a state of body.

4. Look at yourself as a whole person. Choose not to focus on specific body parts.

5. Surround yourself with positive people.

6. Shut down those voices in your head that tell you your body is not 'right' or that you are a 'bad' person.

7. Wear clothes that are comfortable and that make you feel good about your body.

8. Become a critical viewer of media messages, including social media.

9. Do something kind for yourself, something that lets your body know you appreciate it.

10. Use the time and energy that you might have spent worrying about food to help others.

Notes

Week 15:
My values and why they are important

Values are beliefs that guide us. They help us to determine what is important to us. Values describe the individual qualities that we live by. They lead us into action. They make us the person we are, and they direct us towards the person we want to be. They define how we treat ourselves and others.

This next exercise will get you thinking about the values that are meaningful to you. It is good to question your values because if you find yourself stepping outside of them going through life, you will find you are going against yourself. Do you want to go against the things you value? As you get older you will find yourself coming back to the things you value the most. These values can change, but many of them will last a lifetime.

Take a look at the following list. As you read through the words, circle the ones that stand out to you the most. Don't overthink it. Don't take a long time over it. Just circle the ones that resonate with you.

	Creativity	Growth
Acceptance		
	Curiosity	Happiness
Accountability		
	Dedication	Harmony
Achievement		
	Dignity	Health
Adaptability		
	Discipline	Honesty
Awareness		
	Empathy	Honour
Communication		
	Empower	Hope
Community		
	Equality	Humility
Compassion		
	Excellence	Imagination
Connection		
	Fairness	Independence
Consistency		
	Family	Inspiring
Conviction		
	Freedom	Integrity
Cooperation		
	Friendship	Joy
Courage		
	Gratitude	Justice

Kindness	Respect	Transparency
Leadership	Responsibility	Truth
Love	Sensitivity	Unity
Loyalty	Service	Wisdom
Motivation	Spirituality	Vision
Peace	Sustainability	
Purpose	Tolerance	

Next, look again at the words you circled. From these, pick out the five that you feel are the most important to you. This can take a bit of time. That's okay!

Now, take your left hand (or, if you are left handed, your right hand), and place it on the page opposite, with your fingers open. Trace around it so that the outline of your hand is on the page. In each finger write one of your chosen words.

My Values

In the spaces below, write a little about why these words are important to you.

1. _____

_____

2. _____

_____

3. _____

_____

4. _____

_____

5. _____

_____

In the next exercise I want to think of someone who is a good friend. Answer the following questions about them.

Why are they your friend?

_____

_____

What would your friend have to do to lose your friendship?

_____

_____

What values do you see in this friend?

_____

_____

Now, look back at the values you see in your friend. This is an interesting exercise because it helps you to think about what it is that is important to you.

Task for the week

As you go through this week, think about the values that are important to you. Think about what you might improve on, things that you want to make sure you bring into your life. Keep these in your attention. You will need them for the final exercise of this book.

If you are interested, the VIA (Values in Action) website offers a free test, including one aimed at young people. After answering a series of questions, they suggest a list of values that are important to you. If you would like to learn more about your values, you can go to their website and take the test. Just remember, a test like that can't be perfect, but it is a fun thing to do, and you might find the results really interesting.

Type the address below into your browser. It will take you directly to the registration.

https://www.viacharacter.org/survey/account/register

A word from your mentor

Taking time to think about your values will help you to question what is important to you. It's good to ask yourself what it is that you value and why. You may find as you get older that your values will shape the kind of work you do and the kind of friends you have. You might find that it's important to you that people share some of your values.

As you grow up you will move from friends and jobs to find things that sit with your values. It may take you a while, but your happiness could rely on it.

Week 16: Bringing it together with my vision board

I am hoping that by the time you get to this exercise you will have had a few thought-provoking moments: chances to reflect on what's going on in your life and to see how the things around you are influencing you. This could be people, school, music, what you eat, the time you go to bed, what you watch etc. I hope by now that you have taken the plunge and tested out some of the advice in this book. I hope you are finding it useful. I wish most of all that you are trying these tasks long enough to see what a difference they are making. Many of the ideas in this book are being tried and tested all the time. I am seeing firsthand how much they are helping young girls just like you.

Now that you are coming to the end of the book, I would like you to do one last thing. This is to make a vision board. Once it is made I want you to put it somewhere visible. It will be something you go to. It will not only remind you of how far you have come, but it will also visualise what you need.

Looking at your vision board every day will keep you focused on where you want to go. And this can be powerful. Vision boards are sometimes made at the beginning of a new year. They can help you get off on the right foot. Of course, they can be done anytime, and making one after these exercises is a great way to finish on something extremely cathartic and creative, capturing how you feel right now and what you see for the months ahead.

Make sure you have a good two to three hours free to make your board. Play some soothing background music: something that gives you a happy feeling. Prepare a few snacks and a drink.

Before you start, do the meditation exercise I showed you in the first week. Take time to let go and quieten your mind. When you are feeling relaxed and peaceful, start your board.

For your board, you will need.

- Stiff card (measurement can be of your choice)

- Old magazines (get them from friends or family, or ask at your local doctor's/dental surgery)

- Glue stick

- Affirmations/quotes. You can write them yourself or print/copy them from the Internet. Borrow quotes from inspirational people

- Scraps of patterned paper or fabric

- Bits and bobs you may have, like buttons, beads, coloured or patterned paper, tissue paper or ribbon

Preparing:

- Look through your old magazines and cut out anything that resonates with you. It can be a colour, an object, a person, an animal, a place, or something from nature—anything that touches you.

- Find images that capture your needs, wants, desires (keep them realistic)

- Take your time. Take as much time as you like

- Write or print out any affirmations or quotes that come to your mind. If you are choosing some on the Internet, you may want to put a value of yours into Google and ask for a quote on that value. Then print it or write it out

When you have a pile of things in front of you, take your board and place it flat on a surface. Put the things you have cut up on to the board. Play about with them and move them around until you are happy with where everything is. They can overlap. You can use cut up bits of paper to fill the gaps or just leave empty spaces. You might find you want to add more to your board over the coming days, so don't feel it has to be full right away. Once you have everything laid out and you are happy with what you see, start sticking your things down with your glue stick. You don't have to take all the pieces off the board. Just lift each piece and stick until all of your bits are stuck down. Make sure nothing will fall when you pick it up.

When it is finished. Take a photograph of your board and print it out. Stick it in your journal on the next page.

Place the board somewhere you will notice it. Hang it on a wall or rest it on a cupboard. Keep it close. Make it the first thing you see when you wake up.

My Vision Board

Task going forward

Look at your board often. Take time to ask yourself if your goals or needs are being met. Measure yourself using the exercises I have given you in this book. If you find that things are not going well in your life, use this book as a toolkit. Take out the tool you need and fix yourself. If you can't fix yourself, then make sure you talk to someone who can help you. Remember that prevention is the key, so don't leave it until you have a broken part. Use the tools every day. Don't fix one thing and then stop. Keep going every day until these tools become your habit. The idea is to make some of these exercises an everyday part of your life.

A word from your mentor

My hope is that you have really enjoyed this introspective journey. If you have completed this course and made it to the very end, then I applaud you! It takes a lot of courage to do stuff like this, and I am so proud of you.

If you found you have done just some of the exercises, I still applaud you. Sticking to something for 16 weeks is time-consuming, so taking just what you need is also a good idea. I am very proud of you.

I thought a lot about what to say to you when I got to the end of this book. I am sad that we have come to the end, but it is never really the end. I believe it is only the beginning. It has been wonderful being your mentor, and I am honoured that you are reading this and may have possibly have reached the end of this 16-week course.

I believe if you have done many of these exercises, then you will have a lot to say. I would like to hear from you. Please email me at hello@nicolalocke.com with your stories. Tell me what this book has helped you with. Have you managed to do all or any of the exercises? Which ones worked best for you? Give me any feedback you can. I would love to hear from you.

I believe that all young girls like you should be getting these kinds of empowerment workshops in school. If everyone had access to these sessions, especially working in groups, all girls would have a much better chance of becoming self-aware and confident, and of building trusting and loyal friendships that will lead to a much happier life.

I hope this book will inspire parents, teachers, educational administrators and mental-health workers to get on board and make these tasks a daily practice, bringing them to the forefront and making prevention a priority.

Thank you again for taking this magnificent journey into the unknown. I wish you a wonderful life.

REMEMBER to always be kind to yourself.

YOUR LOVING MENTOR

Nicola

About the author

Nicola Locke is a creative and inspirational youth mentor with over 30 years of experience working with children and teens. She has spent most of her life caring about the younger generation. This started way back when she was just 16, mentoring young girls at her local youth club. In 2018 she decided to focus on developing workshops for young girls as she could see how they were increasingly facing serious problems that they were unable to solve by themselves.

She could see that girls were becoming trapped in a competitive and anxious world which was causing them to become more isolated and unhappy. Through her direct work with young girls, she had firsthand experience of the major challenges they were encountering. She could see the epidemic this country was facing due to a lack of resources.

In early 2019 her workshops were born. They have been a success, with a clear message that young girls need all the help they can get. It is apparent to Nicola that not enough is being done for young girls, especially the girls who are on the borderline of emotional and mental health issues. With the demand for schools to deal with 'major' problems, these girls are getting left behind. Nicola believes that if prevention is not put into place many more young girls are going to suffer unnecessarily.

For Nicola, it is not a matter of waiting any longer. It is time to build a framework that will help and encourage young girls to start to take on responsibility of looking after their well-being and the well-being of all the girls around them. Nicola believes that girls need to be taught how to observe themselves closely so that they can work out how to change negative patterns and habits. She feels it is important for girls to look deeper at themselves and their motivations. When girls understand that they too are causing the problems, they see that they can make a positive change. In the workshops, Nicola deliberately sets tasks which challenge girls to think deeply about how they handle themselves. Nicola believes that this kind of emotional intelligence should be at the forefront of every school curriculum. Her hope is that these girls will complete the tasks and pass them on to others who are in need.

Visit Nicola's website at https://www.nicolalocke.com
Email Nicola at hello@nicolalocke.com

Resources:

You can copy these addresses into your Google browser on any phone or computer.

Childline

Childline is a 24-hour free service. You can call the Childline phone number below at any time it is free. You can use Childline for anything related to your health and well-being. If you are worried or scared about something please call them. This line is open to any concerns no matter how big or small. Talking to someone can put your mind at ease. They are anonymous and non-judgemental.

Childline call: 0800 1111

Use the child-line website to find out any information/advice:
https://www.childline.org.uk

Keeping safe online.

This is a UK-based website giving advice on safe internet use. It is designed to help young people.
www.saferinternet.org.uk

Young Minds

Young Minds is another organisation that can be very helpful.
https://youngminds.org.uk

This is a direct connection to bullying.
https://youngminds.org.uk/find-help/feelings-and-symptoms/bullying/

If you need urgent help text YM to 85258
All texts are answered by trained volunteers, with support from experienced clinical supervisors.
Texts are free from EE, O2, Vodafone, 3, Virgin Mobile, BT Mobile, GiffGaff, Tesco Mobile and Telecom Plus.

Eat well guide

NHS (National Health Service) website
www.nhs.uk

This link will take you directly to the NHS eat well guide:
https://www.nhs.uk/live-well/eat-well/the-eatwell-guide/

Beating Eating Disorders

Beat is there to help you if you have any problems regarding concerns about eating disorders.

Call: 0808 801 0711
Website: www.beateatingdisorders.org.uk

Online grooming and sexting advice.

This website was set up by a mum who lost her son to online grooming. Although it is very sad that this happened, this mum did not want it to happen to anyone else, which is why she made this website available.

www.breckfoundation.org

Calm Harm App

This is an app that you can download on to your phone.
www.calmharm.co.uk

Calm Harm provides tasks to help you resist or manage the urge to self-harm. You can make it private by setting a password, and personalise the app if you so wish. You will be able to track your progress and notice change. Please note the app is an aid in treatment but does not replace it.

Taken from calmharm.co.uk

Acknowledgements:

I'd like to thank Shelly Wilson for being a great mentor, for getting me started and motivating me to take on this very important book. Tom Locke, thank you for editing my first draft, for all of your support and patience during the process and for, most of all, believing in me, and pushing me until the very end. Alison Vina, thank you for editing my second draft and for all your input and expertise. It's made all the difference. Michelle and Kyra Hickman, thank you for taking the time to read the book and providing me with your honest and accurate feedback. Kyra Hickman, another big thank you for coming to my workshops and being an example of the positive results. You are a special young girl and your courage will take you far. Katy Biggs and Jane Harman, thank you for your trust in me, and you're honesty. Monalisa Gondosari, thank you for all your great illustrations. Grace and Molly Locke, thank you for being my inspiration.

Notes

Notes

Notes

Notes

Notes

Notes

Printed in Great Britain
by Amazon